Dying to Live?

Dying to Live?

A Christian Approach to the
Matter of Mortality

Kenneth Wilson

 EPWORTH

British Library Cataloguing in Publication data

A catalogue record for this book is available
from the British Library

978 0 7162 0643 9

First published in 2008
by Epworth
4 John Wesley Road
Werrington
Peterborough PE4 6ZP

Typeset by Regent Typesetting, London
Printed and bound in the UK by
MPG Books Ltd, Bodmin, Cornwall

Contents

Preface

This is a cheerful book. Above all, it is an honest book. My purpose in writing is to nourish Christian faith and stimulate a theological contribution to public conversation by setting human life in its fullest perspective, which will therefore necessarily and quite naturally include God and death. In the course of living a normal, healthy, responsible life, every person experiences death and dying in many dimensions, in many ways and in many contexts. There is the loss of a child, the death of a parent, abortion, violent death, sudden death, resentful death, suicide, just possibly voluntary euthanasia and, let us never forget, the normal, gracious, peaceful relapse into Lethe slumber. It is my intention to attempt to come to terms with some of these in what follows.

Christian faith, while never seeking death for its own sake, nevertheless recognizes that the fact of death may be a welcome feature of living. We accept that death is inseparable from life. The sense we make of life *includes* death: one cannot be understood without the other. Indeed, in a profound sense (which to some may appear paradoxical), the Christian faith is stimulated and nourished by the fact of death: without death there would be no faith. Were it not the case that Jesus died as he did, the possibilities and hopes of the Christian faith would not have emerged as they have into the conversation of the generations.

Yet, of all the major religions, the Christian tradition is both most enraged by and most comfortable with death, notwithstanding the paradoxical fact that without death the Christian can make no sense of life. It is through the angst of this apparent confusion and its real sadness that Christian faith is most expressive of the ordinary experience of every human person, in tune with what we call the natural world and which in Christian faith we rightly call Creation.

Cicero, the great Roman lawyer and orator, lost his cousin Lucius by suicide in about 65 BC. Lucius was not only a very good friend, he was also Cicero's indispensable right-hand man in his risky but successful prosecution of Verres, the violent spoliator of the people of the Roman province of Sicily and who, because of his wealth and family connections, believed himself beyond the law. Cicero was deeply affected by the loss and wrote to his friend Atticus: 'Knowing me as well as you do, you can appreciate better than most how deeply my cousin Lucius's death has grieved me, and what a loss it means to me both in public and private life. All the pleasure that one human being's kindness and charm can give another I had from him.'[1] We have all, I expect, endured that vivid sense of loss.

Yet the Christian tradition has more to say, much more. My father died suddenly when I was 16 years old. He died in a hotel room by himself when he was away from home on business. My mother was alone at home and received the message by telephone; I was also elsewhere away from home and was similarly informed by telephone. I packed my things, caught the bus and took the train back home. I can remember very clearly working out on the journey that I was going to take steps to ensure that I would never be hurt again. There were three aspects to this as far as I could see. First, I would never again put my trust in anything or anyone. Second, I would in the future rely on myself for survival. Third, 'love', whatever that was, was out of the question because it demanded a commitment that was always going to result in disappointment and betrayal.

Of course, it was not like that. Many people had a role in ensuring that it was not so. My mother, obviously herself distressed, needed support, as I did. We had the good fortune to have a simply marvellous Methodist minister, the Reverend W. T. Tilsley, who actually knew what it was to *be* a priest and pastor; he took my angry questioning seriously. A distinguished professor of semitic languages and Methodist minister,

Christopher North, decided it was time I learned Hebrew; and the then headmaster of Kingswood School, A. B. Sackett, took the time and trouble to involve me in thoughtful and unthreatening conversation. To all this should be added a host of other influences – teachers, friends and neighbours – whose encouragement and shared exuberance gave me plenty of food for thought. And then there were books, music, the world of art, walking in the mountains, thinking and conversation.

Strange as it may seem, over the course of time I have come to understand that that awful experience of death and dying was the stimulating condition of my awareness of the need for giving and receiving love. Falling in love, marriage, children, the demands of the intellectual life, teachers and teaching, colleagueship, the interest provoked by moral perplexity and spiritual concern, all led me to draw on the riches of human enquiry in the widest sense and the Christian tradition in particular. In fact, it might even have been this experience of death which prompted the response that I should spend much time trying to work out whether I had any faith, what that faith amounted to, and whether it was worth anything. The attempt is ongoing. Most of the time I believe that I have some faith, and realize that I am grateful to my father, among a host of others, for that.

It has taken me a long time to get round to writing this book, but in a sense it is the result of my train journey home from Stockport to Bangor in August 1953. It is a book that I have even now tried to write slowly because I think, if it is to be useful, it is a book that also asks to be read slowly. I have not resorted to the approach of Wittgenstein, who employed assiduous punctuation in order to draw attention to this on the page. He remarked, 'I really want my copious punctuation marks to slow down the speed of reading. Because I should like to be read slowly.'[2]

Life is not open to be 'read' in a moment.

Feast of Thomas Aquinas, priest, philosopher,
teacher of the faith

Time Enough: The *Nunc Dimittis*

The spectre of death

Death is always with us, so it is said – and with justice. And very soon we shall be able to access it at the touch of a switch if Herr Tilmann Schneider, a former producer in German television, has his way. He has announced a new 24-hour channel, Eos TV, named after the Greek goddess of the dawn. The channel will focus exclusively on programmes that deal with ageing, death and dying, and work in close co-operation with the German Funeral Directors Association. As Herr Schneider says, there were in Germany almost 150,000 more deaths than births in 2005–06, with an estimated 2.1 million older people receiving professional care. If you add to this number the families of these people, we are talking of a vast market with a huge potential to attract advertising revenue.[3] I can't wait to view it! Herr Schneider has a point: death is big business. But more to the point, it is also a matter of personal concern which offers, if approached with sensitivity informed by Christian wisdom and understanding, to transform our response to life.

'Man that is born of a woman hath but a short time to live, and is full of misery.'[4] That is one way of looking at the matter of life when regarded from the purely human perspective; it is one that is familiar from the Book of Common Prayer. But it most certainly does not contain the whole truth. On the other hand, the parallel claim that 'In the midst of life we are in death'[5] is true and its significance needs to be taken into account if we are to live lives that are 'good and acceptable and perfect' (Romans 12.2). The thought of living a perfect life is a challenging prospect but, as de Caussade wisely remarked, were it impossible our Lord would not have commanded us to live one after the example of our heavenly Father (Matthew 5.48). If we are to come to grips with such a demanding perspective, we have some work to do.

The spectre of our death always haunts us; it can fill us with an unsettling fear, most especially if we do not face up to it. Fear, as Augustine of Hippo asserts, is an imperfection that arises from the human failure to 'let go' and set our hearts on what we aspire to. Only by thus 'letting go' will we find ourselves and learn to ground our lived experience in God's love, thereby beginning to enjoy the energizing freedom that comes from loving the world and other people that God calls us to in creation.

Yet we should not dismiss the experience of fear as if it were always a bad teacher; it can be a blessed thing, for it reminds us of the limited period of our mortal life that is open to us to learn to live freely. In de Caussade's picture of the Christian life, since there is never any certainty concerning our eternal destiny, there is an appropriate and, therefore, beneficent fear that is 'holy' and 'filial' and which necessarily and usefully comes to us all. We are, he advises, neither to encourage it nor avoid it: everything must be accepted as coming from God. And yet, notwithstanding the reality of fear, we can have confidence as we approach death. 'At the sight of death, fear should be united with confidence, but the latter ought to predominate.'[6]

I am reminded of a prayer that we frequently find in late medieval books of hours, those prayer manuals in which lay people adapted the traditions of monastic spiritual practice for their use. These beautifully illustrated books follow the familiar pattern of the monastic life, but to the printed text the owners would often add in their own handwriting personal prayers concerning their own deaths or in memory of the death of friends and relatives.

I beseche the lorde have mercy on me a wreche and synnere, but yet Lord I am thy creature and for thy precious passion save me and kepe me from all perell bodily and gostely.[7]

The perfect life is one in which confidence in God's love has overcome the natural fear of death and most particularly the ever-present fear of God's justice. This is so as far as it goes, but it is far more than this as we shall see.

Experience, however, tells us that if and when, as is frequently the case, the fear of death comes to take a front seat in a person's life, it is always debilitating and can have a serious effect on one's driving. It is often a perspective of 'middle age' (a spiritual condition which may strike an individual at any age!) for this is the time of life when we are tempted to concentrate on the rear mirror and begin to believe that all our future lies behind us. As we perceive it, middle age kicks in when we feel that all life's substantive choices – friends, education, career, marriage and choice of lifestyle – are behind us and we do not like what we anticipate for the future. We are tempted to waste time raking over the coals of the cooling fires of our lives, looking for a flame by which to warm ourselves. How many of us, I wonder, come to share the experience of Virgil, as Dante puts it at the beginning of *The Divine Comedy*? He sets out on the journey through the *Inferno* conscious of the traumatic prospect that faces him:

> Midway on our life's journey, I found myself
> In dark woods, the right road lost.[8]

Conventionally now we talk of a mid-life crisis when we become aware of issues we recognize we should have faced up to before. Who are we? Where are we going? What are we doing? How did we get into this predicament? What's life all about, if anything? Have we time to deal with all the many questions that arise spontaneously in our minds? Perhaps not – perhaps we have left it too late! We feel ourselves hemmed into a tight corner by circumstances beyond our control, with no future but a rapid acceleration of time as we run downhill through gathering threatening shadows towards the mysterious darkness of death. Those once-distant horizons, which once seemed decades away, far beyond even our imagining, begin to take grotesque forms as they emerge through the mist and come to take possession of our ambitions.

False hopes

In our anxiety we entertain false hopes: we pose to ourselves and to the world impossible questions: How can I extend my life? Can I at least prolong life? How can I avoid death? Can I avoid death? To what or to whom do I turn now? Is there a way out? Of course, there is no way out at all. As one might put it colloquially, 'It is too late to drain the swamp when one is up to one's armpits in alligators.' With luck, or as I would prefer to say with God's grace, we may be reminded of more generous perspectives and ask ourselves the more reasonable questions, How do we make the most of the time left to us, however much or little that is? What next? What lies ahead? And there is, of course, for every Christian, that teasing question, What must I do to be saved? Learning to answer this question properly understood transforms the perspective in which we search for the possibility of meaning and purpose in life. But more of this below.

Health and safety regulations, and more particularly their interpretation by petty officials, can smack of the worst forms of unthinking bureaucracy and appear thoroughly stupid. One headteacher banned conkers because of the risk of injury; another required neckties to be replaced by the clip-on variety in case a child were to be strangled; a third banned making daisy chains because of the danger of infection. A clown has been required to stop inviting children to chase bubbles in case they fall over. And we are all familiar with the notice in cloakrooms by hot-water taps, 'Beware. This water may be hot'; and the printed notice on packets of nuts, 'This packet may contain nuts'. However, the contemporary, frequently exasperating obsession with health and safety does underline one sensible, indeed vital dimension of all planning for the future: when we embark upon any enterprise, whether that be an expedition, a holiday, or a new course of study, we would be wise to prepare a risk analysis. But if this is so when we are considering a holiday on the borders of Eritrea and Somalia, a heart bypass, a career change from the financial world of the City to self-employment as a potter, or deciding to run in on gardening, or whatever. The gift of wisdom and understanding that comes alongside the effort is in itself reward indeed. In committing ourselves to the business of coming to terms with mortality we discover that death offers us life in all its completeness and finality. As we come to terms with it we implicitly enter into the freedom of life itself in all its fullness.

It is true, of course, that the hard work may come to us as suffering because we often experience any work as suffering, but without it we should never be stimulated to accept the offer of freedom. This is very much a counter-cultural comment. Wittgenstein saw it as a dimension of education sadly lacking in his time. He noted in 1948:

> I think the way people are educated nowadays tends to diminish their capacity for suffering. At present a school is reckoned good 'if the children have a good time'. And that used *not* to be the criterion. Parents want their children to grow up like themselves (only more so), but nevertheless subject them to an education *quite* different from their own. Endurance of suffering isn't rated highly because there is supposed not to be any suffering – really it's out of date.[10]

Nothing could be further from the truth; far from being 'out of date', suffering is a necessary condition of every educational process, especially when one realizes that learning is a lifelong process. We are not educated in order that we may suffer, but educated so that we may understand and bear suffering – and death – in such a way as to triumph over them. Elizabeth Barrett Browning (1806–61) gets it right when she says:

> Knowledge by suffering entereth;
> And life is perfected by Death.[11]

I do not wish by this for one moment to diminish the pain of suffering or the sadness which death brings; simply to put it into the grand perspective of more abundant life with God, which is what death offers.

There are very many people who do suffer terribly and who live with the real threat and fear of an imminent violent death, one of which they are daily very conscious, but about which they believe they can do very little or nothing. In a survey of 2,000 people in Iraq regarding the quality of life four years after the overthrow of Saddam Hussein in March 2003, 86 per cent reported that they lived each day in fear of their own violent death or that of a member of their family.[12] One cannot ignore that, or indeed the threat of death by AIDS in Zambia. The people of the ravaged country of Zimbabwe have the lowest life expectancy in the world, and experience an inflation rate of many thousands per cent. It is estimated that 85 per cent of the population of that country live in poverty and, at the time of writing, in fear of the so-called security forces.[13] Indeed these terrible circumstances, or conditions very like them, are shared by many citizens in many countries of the world, from Gaza to Chechnya, from Sri Lanka to Haiti, from Somalia to Colombia, not to mention some of the homeless who sleep on the streets of Mumbai, New York and London.

Those of us who live in an apparently more settled environment will hardly envy these people their situation, yet looked at from another perspective, these are the very people who are liberated to live as fully as they can day by day. It is a humiliating realization. As Deutero-Isaiah had it:

> But he was wounded for our transgressions,
>   crushed for our iniquities;
> upon him was the punishment that made us whole,
>   and by his bruises we are healed.[14]

Would to God that we were driven by the vision of perfection to fight alongside the deprived and fearful, for we might glimpse then just what Deutero-Isaiah's profound insight implies. We might even come to see how absolutely vital it is to the business of living well that we recognize that in principle we all share in the same situation of each person whose life is under threat: this thought is not redolent of romantic sentimentality, but grounded in theologically sensitive reason.

8

This is what Jesus draws our attention to in his parable about the prosperous farmer and landowner (Luke 12.16–21). A very rich man had a quite superb harvest. Lucky man! What could he do with the produce? It was more than he had room for in his present buildings. 'I know what I'll do,' he said, 'I'll pull down my barns and build some much larger ones; that's what I'll do. This will give me decent room to store all my wealth. Then I can sit back and enjoy myself until the next harvest comes around.' There is just a hint here of the unfortunate man who buried his talent and hoped for the best; but Jesus does not condemn this farmer as a bad man, nor does he say that his decision to build bigger barns was mistaken. He simply comments that he was unwise and should have taken stock of his total circumstances. 'What a silly attitude,' says Jesus, 'the very night on which he made what he quite understandably believed to be a wise decision, he died.' And he had not taken that into account.

The point is not that he was obviously wrong to take stock of the situation and deal with it; he did have a large crop and may well have needed bigger barns. His failure lay in the fact that he did not take account of the *total* situation that he faced. Like every human being, he was a soul who lived in the presence of God, but he neglected to take this fact into account in the pursuit of what he believed to be the more immediate demands of preserving his wealth. In loving the world, he thought he could put God aside temporarily. Not so, never. No circumstance can ever make sense of the idea that we can save our lives by roofing it – or burying it. The treasure of a life is that it should be spent wisely, fruitfully and worthily. We are all, every moment of our lives, in a situation that demands that we take account of our life here and now *in toto*, which will necessarily therefore assume that life is lived in the presence of God. That this is possible is the promise of the gospel.

The apostle Paul sets the whole thing in perspective in what we know as his Letter to the Romans.

I appeal to you therefore, brothers and sisters, by the mercies of God, to present your bodies as a living sacrifice, holy and acceptable to God, which is your spiritual worship. Do not be conformed to this world, but be transformed by the renewing of your minds, so that you may discern what is the will of God – what is good and acceptable and perfect. (Romans 12.1–2)

Paul is not talking of some future prospect. 'I do hope that in due course you will get round to presenting your bodies as a living sacrifice.' It is, after all, a *living* sacrifice of which Paul is writing. So it is a here-and-now actuality that Paul is calling for. This is what life is like for the Christian, he says: living a sacrificial life that is holy and acceptable to God. Paul, according to the translation of the Authorised Version, addresses the feuding and divided Church of Corinth with the astonishing but encouraging instruction in the context of a blessing: 'Finally, brethren, farewell. Be perfect, be of good comfort, be of one mind, live in peace; and the God of love and peace shall be with you.'[15] That word 'perfect' again! It is not a depressing but a stimulating thought, one that is life-giving, fulfilling and affirming of the life-in-Trinity that God offers here and now to the world of human being in Christ through the Holy Spirit.

The gift of death

But it does not, of course, always seem like that. Let's turn to a most difficult question. The manner of a person's dying, longevity or the lack of it, the apparent injustice of some deaths, often leads to despair, frustration, pain and guilt on the part of those who remain. The death of a promising young student through misadventure, the shocking murder of a priest, a cot death, or the sudden fatal illness of a young mother, especially stir our dark imagining and disturb the mind. Such circumstances not surprisingly cause some insufferable torments that can test faith to breaking point. If God cared, God would have done something about it! Rather than looking at human life as a whole, including God the Redemptive Creator, we are inclined at such moments to look towards the hoped-for promise that will come from building bigger barns or, in this case better science, more investment in education, greater political authority and more creative technology. No wonder that the optimistic predictions of some about life in the future are grasped for with desperate hope. Surely stem-cell research, nanotechnology, better resuscitation procedures, faster communication systems together with new drugs and new means of delivering them will extend life for all to at least 120 years, if not more, over the course of this twenty-first century. But would this – *per impossibile* – even if it came about, put death out of mind? Would death by such developments be put to death? Not on your life; of course not!

I was struck by Wittgenstein's aphorism when I read it: 'The horrors of hell can be experienced within a single day; that's plenty of time.'[16] It is; the depths of hellish pain can be endured in a day. Günter Grass offers such a perspective in his autobiography.[17] Heaven, on the other hand, requires a lifetime, but a lifetime can be of any length: every life is complete in itself. A lifetime is time enough to be equipped to enjoy God's loving presence, because to be born is to *be* in God's presence. Longevity is not the issue.

In any case, is that what we want? Karel Capek's fine short story, 'The Makropulos Case', was made into a marvellous opera of the same title by Janacek. It tells the story of Elina Makropulos. Her father, a court physician, tries out on her an elixir of life. It works, it is wonderful; life in perpetuity is not only possible, it is realized. We've cracked it; death has been defeated! But not so, it appears. At the time of the action of the story, Elina has lived under a number of aliases; she is 342, fed up to the nines with the boredom of it all and anxious to die. She summons up the courage to refuse the elixir and achieves her purpose; she dies. Moreover, a brave young woman, despite protests, destroys the elixir. Most of us surely think this young woman had good common sense! As Bernard Williams writes in concluding an essay on this subject, we are 'lucky in having the chance to die'.[18]

My understanding of our mortal condition is that, contrary to Bernard Williams, death is not to be attributed to good luck, but to our good God who in Christ reveals the true value and nature of death. I suggest, therefore, that notwithstanding the circumstances, whatever the period of a person's life, long or brief, whatever the tragedy accompanying the death, there was and is time enough for the person to know God and God's love. This must seem unfeeling and unhelpful to persons without faith, and indeed to many who believe they have faith. But from the Christian perspective one knows that there is always time. Indeed, let's put it into perspective and in figurative language. Can you imagine turning up at the pearly gates and saying to God, 'But you didn't give me time!' Or God saying, 'I need more time to prepare for your arrival.' To talk in such a way is a quite natural reaction to our own fear that on reflection we had not made good use of the time available to us, but that is rather a different matter and something that I shall want to consider later.[19] We will do well to keep in mind Heidegger's sensitive remark, 'As soon as man comes to life, he is at once old enough to die.'[20]

To take another aspect of concern, it is not true, for example, that one has made all the choices that are life-giving by the time one is middle aged. It is not even true in the present socio-economic climate that one has necessarily finished one's career choices by the time one is 50 or even 60 years of age.[21] Many – even most – may have done; in fact, however, the speed of socio-economic change combined with increased longevity and good health is such that one is likely to have to re-equip oneself for employment several times during one's lifetime. We can take seriously the possibility of productive work until well into our seventies or even eighties. And why not!

Yet from the Christian perspective, continuous employment with regular new opportunities for change are not the key things to grasp after in relation to one's knowledge of and love for God. That comes from the simple desire for God in whatever circumstance one finds oneself. Whether he was travelling by ship, arrested and taken to Rome for trial and imprisoned, whether he was in dispute with Peter, or encouraging the communities of the faithful with which he was familiar to wait on God, Paul was able to practise the presence of God. It was not that he consciously called God to mind at every turn, but that the habit of faith in the risen Christ so informed his way of living that he *in fact* gave thanks at all times because he knew full well not so much his love of God as God's love of him and all people. Confidence overcame fear.

I shall have more to say about the habit of wanting God later; suffice it to say at this juncture that Aquinas' emphasis upon it as the consequence of the practice of the faith is of profound importance if we are to be persons formed by faith.

Jesus whom we call the Christ: time enough

The life of Jesus is the particular case for the Christian to consider. We know little about this man Jesus. But of two things we can be certain: his life was short, his ministry even shorter; but his impact on the future history of humankind immeasurably great. Born in a minor part of the Roman Empire into a very ordinary family, the background from which Jesus came was inauspicious, especially when looked at from a purely socio-economic point of view. Was he a carpenter? We don't know, though there is a tradition that suggests that he was. But even if Jesus did learn the trade of carpentry, what social standing was accorded to a carpenter in the maelstrom of first-century Jewish society? A carpenter might be regarded as useful, but hardly a prosperous trendsetter, one imagines. Jesus seems to have been a serious-minded chap, a committed fellow, whose stature and wisdom were admired, according to Luke: he was, as we might say, 'a good lad'.

Yet according to the many traditions found in the Gospels, all sorts of things were said about him in his childhood which were very puzzling to his parents and to anyone else who overheard them. Simeon thought his time had come when he set eyes on Jesus – this was the Lord's Messiah! Anna recognized in him a person for whom she should praise God. Herod, the King of the Jews, feared for his own future when he was told of the rumours about the birth of another King of the Jews: he, Herod, was surely the King of the Jews!

We do not know whether any of these stories represent real events at the start of Jesus' life, or whether they were conventional expectations of the ordinary religious Jew who looked daily for the possibility of the fulfilment of God's promises in the scriptures. The period of which we are speaking in the early Roman Empire was clearly a rumour-ridden environment full of sound and fury usually signifying nothing. Something exciting was just around the corner, or so many believed.

Certainly, Luke's Gospel has it that Jesus' parents were devout Jews who went annually to Jerusalem for the festival of the Passover. They presented Jesus in the Temple for their purification according to the Law of Moses. On another occasion, when he was 12 and his parents were on their way home, his absence was unnoticed among the perhaps substantial group of pilgrims with whom for purposes of security they had made the journey. After a day's journeying they became aware that he was missing, and returned to Jerusalem to look for him. And there he was, arguing – at any rate discussing and reasoning – with the rabbis who seemed to find what he had to say intriguing and worth paying attention to. Again we cannot be sure of any of this, or indeed how exceptional such precocity was. Certainly it was not unique; in contrast for example, to the Roman pattern that associated wisdom with old age and experience, youth was no bar to authority among the Jews.[22]

Against such an unpropitious and insignificant background, no doubt including much more about which we know nothing, it was not until he was about 30 years of age that Jesus 'began his work'.[23] And either it was all over in one year or at most in three. Snuffed out in the prime of life, we might say – but not a bit of it. Notwithstanding various statements scattered in the four Gospels, it is not clear whether we can with any confidence form a firm view of what sense he may have had of his own destiny. Did he know that he was the Son of God, and if he did what *on earth* – I use the phrase advisedly, given his conventional Jewish upbringing – could he have meant by it? Did he believe that he was called to be the Saviour of the World, the Messiah, the Son of Man? Who knows? Certainly it attracted discussion among some of his peers. 'Who does this upstart think he is? We know who he is, he's the son of Joseph the carpenter, born in Nazareth. Nothing good ever came from that place!' Scholars have argued about it, do argue about, and will argue about it for ever.

Does it matter? Well, yes and no. Yes, in the sense that it will always be important to argue about it and to test the evidence, such as it is. No, in the sense that what he thought about his own status is irrelevant against what, by his life and death, teaching and conversation, he actually achieved. Indeed, the one vital feature of the whole Gospel story seems to me to be that in whatever way he came to hold the view, he was utterly convinced by and responded to the thought that God was present in the world as Redemptive Creator and ever-present Lord. And therefore, of course, with him and with every other person. Nothing, he believed, could expunge the reality of God's giving of God's self in creation for the world's perfection. That absolute commitment and the relationship that it implied provided the possibility of salvation for all; it conditioned everything that a human being should do, if he or she was to know the sense, meaning and purpose of life. It conditioned profoundly Jesus' sense of the value and character of his own life. Indeed, he saw his own life and all human life as life-for-others, if it was to be of value to himself and to God.

Death as Jesus saw it – the acceptance of the reality of death – was the foundation of the possibility of true life. Christians have proclaimed ever since that the truth of his understanding of death and of his faith in God is to be found in his resurrection and ascension. So much out of so little? Precisely: there is always time enough, as those wonderfully suggestive and intriguing last words that John puts in the mouth of Jesus on the Cross imply: 'It is finished.'[24] And it is for all of us, which is why Jesus taught his disciples to share in his prayer, '*Our* Father'.

I wonder what we make of Jesus' last moments on the cross. It could be said that it was just at that time that Jesus made plain to us his inexhaustibly gracious love. He was more concerned for those around him than for himself, in pain though he must have been and bowed down under the apparent disgrace of a criminal's public crucifixion. Moreover, deserted by his friends, taunted by the disbelieving crowd in holiday mood, who only days before had welcomed him with palms and psalms, he had time for others. And the significance of the word 'time' in that sentence must not be missed: he had *time* for others! Time indeed is of the essence of the situation, for it was the dying thief who on the cross – a man justly condemned for a crime he had committed (as far as we know) – asked to be remembered by Jesus. And what did Jesus reply? 'Today you will be with me in Paradise.' Today. It is never too late; there is always time. And the time is now.

That seems right, and we find it relatively easy to accept it and see the point of it. There is always time, not only for God but also for us. Even at the last moment, one's mind may clear, one's sense of guilt or regret, ambition or hope, furnish the need for salvation, and one may turn to God and pray to be remembered. It is never too late. But dare one say, It is never too soon? That is harder, much harder, but I believe one can. To put it in context, can you imagine a young child turning up to meet St Peter and being rejected by him on behalf of God? 'Sorry, you've come too soon; we're not ready for you. You are only 12 weeks, 12 months, 12 years old; you have got a lot more to learn before you can take up a place here.' I can't. Of course, from our point of view we have a tragic loss to come to terms with. But we can be helped by the thought that God can never be caught out; it is never too soon for God.

The impatience and frustration of humankind are in strong contrast to the patience and courtesy of God as revealed in Christ. Why isn't the world as we would like it to be? And how, if only we had had the chance, we would have made it so much better! For us there is never enough time, or there is too much time. But for God there is always time, given the timelessness of God's being and essential nature of God's relationship with the world of his creation. But we want to get on with 'converting the world'.

It is a natural mistake to confuse what it is to *be* a missionary church with the tawdry, tiresome business of counting heads. (Aren't *you* tired of filling in those forms, and turning up to those meetings where your performance is appraised?) To *be* a missionary church is to share in the redemptive creativity of God's relationship with the world and to share in the delight of conversation with a world which bears God's stamp. *Bearing* witness is the process by which we do just that: namely, suffer with Christ for the world's sake in self-giving, other-affirming life. When we have once recognized the reality of God's living, redemptive creativity in the world of our experience, we will be willing to accept our share of responsibility and set about the business of living out the truth in patience without anxiety or fear.

Simeon was right; he did not ask for more time to see the whole thing worked out in detail. When he saw Jesus, he recognized the power of God in God's creation and was able to die in peace. If it is not part of our personal tradition to say daily the Office of Evening Prayer and therefore the *Nunc Dimittis*, we should regularly use a prayer that expresses similar confident hope and expectation:

Lord, now lettest thou thy servant depart in peace:
According to thy word.

For mine eyes have seen:
Thy salvation;

Which thou hast prepared:
Before the face of all people;

To be a light to lighten the Gentiles:
And to be the glory of thy people Israel.

Glory be to the Father, and to the Son:
And to the Holy Ghost;
As it was in the beginning, is now, and ever shall be:
World without end. Amen.[25]

2

Learning to Die Well: Formation and the Community of Faith

The Victorians, as did the Romans, laid great emphasis on 'dying well'; for both Romans and Victorians death was something that one did rather than something that simply happened to one; death was an active process. Moreover, the manner of someone's death could reveal the person's true character.[26] The theme has been a matter of some importance throughout the history of the Church and is a vital element of Christian spirituality. Death matters!

However, it may be that it is in reaction to this philosophy that there has been much less focus upon death and dying in recent times. Many factors have tended to diminish its immediacy. Families are scattered and so it is unusual to find them gathered to support a dying person, though common for them to share in the funeral service. Most deaths are in hospital or nursing home rather than in the family home. Moreover, life expectancy has increased, with the consequence that a family will experience death less frequently than was the case and therefore will be less conversant with traditional practice. Furthermore, most people die drugged and in an unconscious state. And then, of course, in the West at any rate and Europe in particular, there is the continuing decline in the practice of Christian faith, not to mention the reduction in the number of clergy of all denominations.

Of course, many of the practical matters associated with death and its consequences continue to be recognized as issues for the exercise of personal responsibility. Everyone knows that it is important to make a will so that one's wishes in respect of organ donation and the business of inheritance are easy for the heirs. It is commonly accepted that one should clear debts as far as possible, and make plain what arrangements one wants for the funeral. The constantly changing perspective of legislation affecting such matters as death duties gives an edge to one's thinking if one is a British citizen! Longevity has brought other practical issues such as living wills, assisted dying and euthanasia to the fore.[27] This is all fine; they are all matters that should receive attention. However, it is my belief that for the Christian it is important in the much broader context of Christian faith to consider what it means to die well, and part of the work of the family and the faith community is to help a person to die well.

Death: the basic sacrament

The term 'die well' may seem to smack of contradiction. How can one die *well*? Surely if one was well, one would not be ill, let alone die! But this is just the point. We can die well, though the significance of the statement needs to be unpacked. Ladislaus Boros talks of death as the basic sacrament, mysteriously present in other sacraments. By this he means that the grace of God is present in the moment of death, with the potential lively opportunity that the person will recognize and wholeheartedly accept the love of God that has in fact accompanied him or her throughout life. Life is transformed by death such that its divine nature is revealed without question. He writes:

> Death is man's first completely personal act, and is, therefore, by reason of its very being, the centre above all others for the awakening of consciousness, for freedom, for the encounter with God, for the final decision about one's eternal destiny.[28]

To think of death as something which one *does* rather than something which happens *to* one is marvellously encouraging: moreover, to recognize it to be something which one does in the company of others and in the presence of God makes it clear that one can die well or badly. It is a personal action that takes place in community, not a private act. If that is so, it is worth learning to do it well. If we are seriously to take this on board, with all its implications for the way in which we think about our lives, some preliminary work is necessary. There are important dimensions to take into account, so let's begin at the beginning if we can.

The evolution of our understanding of death

It is reasonable to assume that the significance of death only gradually dawned on the human race in the course of evolution. Given that this is so, it is also reasonable to assume that further developments are likely to emerge in our human response to the fact of death. But already, over the relatively brief period of human development, especially over the recent many tens of thousands of years, humankind has recognized that death is a natural phenomenon, a common feature of all forms of life. Indeed, growing awareness of death and its prospective significance for life may have had in the course of evolution an important influence on humankind's growing self-consciousness, and may indeed still have.[29] But death has nevertheless always posed a question to the human mind. What was human life about if it existed for but a few years, only to be swept away in the nonexistence of death? What was the point? The fact that death might be a natural phenomenon seemed to make the problem all the more puzzling. Of course it seems obvious to us, that death is real; what would an alternative look like? One cannot pretend that one is alive when one has died, even if one's friends and family may want to try to do so. However, to recognize the brute fact of death is one thing; to accept it and build it into a positive understanding of life and its possible meaning is quite another. Where did it come from? How did it come about? What explanation could there possibly be for such an unlooked-for dimension of life?

Archaeologists have found that the skeletons in a high proportion of the prehistoric burials they have excavated show evidence of sudden death at a relatively young age. This may have come about through illness, misadventure, accident, as a consequence of attacks by wild animals, or perhaps through what we would now call criminal acts. In fact, as we might say, very few people died of old age. The inference has sometimes been drawn that since death was usually or at least commonly experienced to be the result of accident or mistake, prehistoric people believed it was something that they could and should learn to avoid. It has even been suggested that the belief may have grown up that death was somehow unnatural rather than natural. We know better.

Speculation arising from puzzlement at the fact of death has stimulated theories about the origins of religion. It is commonly assumed that religion emerged as a compensatory system of belief in an afterlife by which to overcome the fear of death – but this is unlikely. There was a belief in continuity of life for a privileged few, as is for example evidenced in the provision of food and wealth for the Pharaohs in the pyramids, or the tribal leaders in the long barrows of Salisbury Plain. But belief in a potential afterlife for all was not a part of early religious belief. Indeed, belief in an afterlife only became central to religion with Christianity in the first century AD. More plausible is the view that people developed religious practices as a means of trying to postpone death, if not actually of overcoming it. If the right potion could be taken, the right words employed, the correct ritual acts performed, then the forces of nature, the gods, could be placated and life extended, even if it did gradually dawn upon the prehistoric imagination to think that death could not be avoided altogether. We know better because we understand without doubt that death is real and natural. In any case, the proportion of prehistoric deaths for which we have evidence from the excavation of burials must be a minuscule set of the total number of deaths: it is impossible to draw firm general conclusions from the slim evidence available.

Marx and Freud produced other theories that have been influential. They both sought to account for the phenomenon of religious belief in practical terms, though in different senses.

Marx believed that religion flourished as a result of collusion between those with political and economic power and those who suffered from their indifferent and selfish behaviour. The persecuted comforted themselves with the thought of 'pie in the sky when you die', while the powerful encouraged this illusion because it kept people docile in their subjection. Freud regarded religion as the fantastic compensating construction of the neurotic condition of humankind in the face of death – useful if untrue because it potentially gave a calming significance to life. But these practical contexts for the emergence of religion have no substance because, as I have said, there is no evidence for the early emergence of belief in life after death.

Far from emerging, therefore, as an illusory means of coping with death and the apparently unreasonable suffering endured by humanity, the contrary seems to be the case: religious belief emerged in human society as a way of explaining the apparently surprising fact of life itself considered as a whole, including death. If death could not be dismissed as the consequence of accident or mistake but had to be accepted as a normal fact of life – of all life – it requires a more serious attempt to understand it, involving in principle life and 'the nature of the universe', an explanation of how things are in the world and where human life fits into this totality.[30] Religious belief developed in response to the intellectual, emotional, moral and spiritual demands for understanding the 'human situation' that arose in the course of everyday life. But in a world where life included death and its naturalness as a given to be accepted, death still had to be explained.

Interpretation, meaning and the facts

Death is indubitably a fact of life, but facts are notoriously slippery and come in all shapes and sizes. Their significance is at least partially determined by the way in which we interpret them and the inferences that we draw from them. It is, for example, a fact that the Soviet empire collapsed in 1989, but what exactly this 'fact' signified and signifies will continue to become clear over the next years and decades. It is very hard, as historians constantly remind us, to determine exactly when the empire fell: it may indeed be a foolish and unanswerable question, one not even worth asking. In a profound sense, we do not even know exactly when it occurred, or what the 'fact' of the collapse of the Soviet empire means. Indeed, the re-emergence of Russian imperial ambitions under President Putin raises the question whether it really collapsed. Undoubtedly, only gradually will we be able to people the 'event' with our interpretations, expectations, predictions and sensible understandings as we engage in the intriguing process of 'making sense of it'. Such enquiring after the 'meaning' of an event is a continuous process that demands keen attention to detail and imagination to place it into the many frameworks in which it is set.

An analogous point can be made given the responses to the fact of death implicit in the several religious traditions of Hinduism, Buddhism, Judaism, Christianity and Islam. The fact of death is undeniable, but what the human world makes of it, what it means for us is only apparent from an examination of the significance attributed to it. Is it part of a long process of reward and punishment involving reincarnation as one moves towards the unfeeling perfection of Nirvana? Is it a porch into a world of delightful pleasure through which one can enter by engaging in dramatic action to please an all-powerful God who above all demands uncritical obedience? And what does 'uncritical obedience' mean in this case?

There again, perhaps death is no more and no less than the end of life? Human beings snuff it; is that all there is to it?[31] In which case of course the more intelligent of us will treat life as a 'jolly' to be enjoyed to the utmost while the opportunity exists. Edith Piaf, 'The Little Sparrow', perhaps best sums up this attitude to life and death in her famous song, *Je ne regrette rien*, 'There's nothing to regret'. However, I regret that there is no space here to discuss the many responses of the other major religions, interesting and important though they are. Certainly, however, the theological and philosophical framework in which one's tradition places it will profoundly influence what one means by 'dying well'. My purpose here is to focus upon the Christian tradition and the way we, from the point of view of our faith, approach the fact of our own mortality. [32]

The Christian understanding of life and death

What story does the Christian religion tell about life and therefore also of death? The biblical framework provided by Judaism gives the key. The book of Genesis tells the story of all creation and therefore all life having begun with the initiative of God. Without God there would simply be nothing. God brought the world into existence through God's Word: God sustains it in existence through the loving-kindness of God's gracious presence. Without life, of course, there would have been no death, and the writer of Genesis explains how life includes death in the story of the Fall.[33] Adam was seduced by Eve to taste the apple of the tree of knowledge in direct violation of the command of God, thus spoiling the world of human endeavour. Humankind therefore incurred God's just punishment of death and human suffering as a consequence. The story was taken up in the Christian tradition. Theologians and believers have wrestled with it ever since and sought to do justice to the human condition by developing the thoughtful doctrine of original sin, with all its implications.[34] It is, for example, an illuminating if depressing reflection that the Hebrew root for 'begin' is the same as the root that means 'spoil'. Surely we are not doomed to spoil everything that God has begun or that we might aspire to begin? Perhaps we are. Personal experience and human history would tend to confirm it. But there is more to say, much more.

Important as the doctrine of the Fall is in the Christian tradition, questions and hopes raised by an understanding of the world as God's creation, the life and work of Jesus Christ, the Living Word of God, the many (equally varied and controversial) claims of religious experience, and the sheer intellectual puzzlement arising from the fact that there is anything at all, are all even more important. All figure in Christianity, and all involve taking seriously the fact of life in death.

Christians believe death to be a blessing, not a curse, because it owes its origin to God. Christians understand God not only to have created the world but also to have accepted responsibility for everything involved in it, its well-being and ultimate perfection, including death. Indeed, the affectionate courtesy with which the God of love addresses the world is summed up for the Christian in the belief that God committed God's self in Christ to declare within the natural world not the fact of death but the reality of life. Living within the Christian tradition points one to the worthwhileness of the struggle, with the paradoxical claim implicit in the Christian tradition that it is through the fact of death as experienced by Christ that God celebrates and points to the reality of life.

God expresses God's self in and through the incarnation of the Living Word whom we call Jesus, the Christ, the Son of God. Jesus lived, taught, suffered and was cruelly crucified in order to liberate humankind into the freedom of God's loving presence, that is, into life itself. Paul puts it this way: '. . . as all die in Adam, so all will be made alive in Christ'.[35] He was raised from the dead, and ascended into heaven in order to show the real nature of creation when life is lived in conscious recognition of God's real presence. In order to come to terms with what God speaks in creation and in Jesus Christ, and to take up our place in the community of faith, it is necessary to accept the fact of our mortality. But if, as our tradition puts it, we follow Christ, 'take up our cross', and take seriously what it means to live in God's world, we shall be inspired to think through, with as much intelligence as we can muster, the fundamental question of why there is anything at all. The whole range of the worlds of human delight – emotional, intellectual, aesthetic, moral and personal – will be engaged in the process if we are to become aware of the nature of our own being and equipped to live day by day with Christ with the encouragement of the Holy Spirit in the presence of God, our Father.[36] The fruit of this is not simply that we shall be able to live life confidently but that we shall also be empowered to enjoy it to the full. In order to be able to do this we shall need to be equipped to explore the one thing that matters; not simply the usefulness, relevance and practical significance of our religion, but its truth. After all, it is the truth of our religion and the reality of God that will matter most to us when we die, and which therefore should matter most to us in our life.

How can the Christian prepare to die well?

Given this perspective on death, to learn to die well is a sensible, life-giving and creative ambition. How does the Christian rightly prepare for it? What resources are available to us, and where do we begin?

Let us first acknowledge that Christianity is uniquely honest in its acceptance of the absoluteness of death when considered as a phenomenon of human life. But as suggested in the previous chapter, we do not understand human life to be exhaustively described from within the set of physical, empirical, scientific frameworks that are open to our inspection. This is so because for the Christian the life of the natural world, including human being, derives its meaning, sense, coherence and value from the fact that it is set also within a larger framework that includes God. Human life is not simply natural, but as natural, also holy and divine. This requires some explanation, but it is essential if we are to understand the full depth and breadth of our humanity and the nature of the world of which we are a part.

The Gospels and Paul's writings are full of the wholeness of this perspective, but it comes through most powerfully in the pseudonymous Second Epistle of Peter. Written in the face of much anxiety about the moral condition of the world in the second century, and in the face of Epicurean and Jewish heretical rejection of an afterlife, the author publicly declares his greater insight:

May grace and peace be yours in abundance in the knowledge of God and of Jesus our Lord.
His divine power has given us everything needed for life and

godliness, through the knowledge of him who called us by his own glory and goodness. Thus he has given us, through these things, his precious and very great promises, so that through them you may escape from the corruption that is in the world because of lust, and may become participants in the divine nature. For this very reason, you must make every effort to support your faith with goodness, and goodness with knowledge, and knowledge with self-control, and self-control with endurance, and endurance with godliness, and godliness with mutual affection, and mutual affection with love. For if these things are yours and are increasing among you, they keep you from being ineffective and unfruitful in the knowledge of our Lord Jesus Christ. For any one who lacks these things is short-sighted and blind, and is forgetful of the cleansing of past sins. Therefore, brothers and sisters, be all the more eager to confirm your call and election, for if you do this, you will never stumble. For in this way, entry into the eternal kingdom of our Lord and Saviour Jesus Christ will be richly provided for you.[37]

From this we may see clearly that to prepare for a good death is a matter first and foremost of leading a good life. Such a life will be lived in full knowledge of the nature of the human–divine world of creation as revealed in Christ, for his life of glory was lived in the real world of human experience and therefore in the presence of God. Moreover, this epistle is not directed to a particular congregation: it is a catholic epistle addressed *urbi et orbi*, 'to the city and the world'. It makes clear that this promise is in principle for all people and all creation; those who are short-sighted should lift their eyes, those who are blind should open them.

As Marmion, the Abbot of Maredsous and a fine writer on the spiritual life, has said:

Holiness, in man, is only possible according to the Divine Plan: to know this plan, to adapt oneself to it is the whole substance of holiness.

This plan consists in calling the human creature to partici-
pate, by the grace of supernatural adoption, in God's own
eternal life.

. . .

Man enters into participation of this Divine life by sanctifying
grace, which, whilst leaving him in his condition of creature,
makes him truly, by adoption, the child of God: the Heavenly
Father encompasses all Christians in an extension of His
Fatherhood in relation to His own Son Jesus Christ.[38]

Now the words 'plan' and 'supernatural' make uncomfortable
reading for me in this context because of what so many imply by
them: they grate on my mind, bringing more heat than light. But
when Abbot Marmion places the life of humankind within the
divine life of God, the Holy Trinity, he is exactly right. In any
case one may be over-sensitive about the use of words. There
are, after all, good plans and bad plans. A bad plan is one fixed
in advance without regard to the evidence and without attention to changing circumstances. Napoleon Bonaparte had such
a plan when attacking Russia in 1812. He was doomed to fail
because he was unwilling to respond to the local circumstances
and take help where it might have been found. He crossed with
his army the newly created frontiers between Lithuania, Poland
and Russia, taking no account of the opportunities which might
have accrued to him as a result of the disenchantment of the
local population that was suspicious of Russian intentions and
might have been willing to look to him for leadership and pro-
tection. Instead, he ignored them and marched straight on to
Moscow, failing even to take account of the prospective threat
to his troops of the harsh Soviet winter.

In respect of the life of faith, the idea of a plan for a person's
life has often been heard to suggest something analogous to just
such a route march, as if one's life was planned out in every detail
and a person could press on without attention to surroundings,
personal or material. There must be no turning to the left or the
right, come hell or high water; that, it is argued by some, is what
is meant by faith if a person is to fulfil their mission and live the

life that God had 'planned' for them. Of course that's rubbish; nothing could be further from the truth. Such a life would be characteristic of a zombie, not the life of any *human* being – let alone a life lived in the faith of Christ. Faith, and therefore one's theological perspective on living in God's good world, must be always developing in the light of new experience.

Faith is no more blind than is intelligent planning! Every good plan will have risk assessments built into it, and be open to the rethinking demanded by fresh information. The flexibility that is built into careful planning will render a resourceful planner capable of taking account of new circumstances and understandings as they arise. God's creative planning, insofar as it is sensible to use such anthropomorphic language, is for a world of constant opportunity and hope for humankind in general, and each human person in particular. To be human is to reflect on the way – more likely the ways – in which we can from our own point of view become conscious of, understand and work with what it means to live out a life in the presence of God who is creatively redemptive. Classical spirituality calls this discernment.[39] God is the constant encourager and illuminator, which is what we mean when we talk of God in terms of the Holy Spirit. 'God is alive and well and lives in Bristol', was the slogan written across the stage of a performance of the rock musical *Hair* in that city many years ago. Indeed, God does live in Bristol; and in Grantham, Baghdad and, notwithstanding all evidence to the contrary, in Darfur too. The freedom to recognize this and to respond by living life accordingly is open to every human person everywhere. It is one aspect of what we mean when we talk of 'becoming human'.

And as for the word 'supernatural', it should be written 'supernatural' (with a hyphen). For when properly interpreted in Christian theology it means 'more deeply and consistently natural' that is, holy and divine. Human life and the world of creation are indeed natural and therefore divine, if only one has the eyes to see. But that requires faith, perhaps. Christians believe human beings to be subjects whose true nature is revealed by the possibility of divine life when considered in relation to God, as we understand him through Christ. The writer has this clearly in his mind when talking with the Gentile Christians of Ephesus:

> So then you are no longer strangers and aliens, but you are citizens with the saints and also members of the household of God, built upon the foundation of the apostles and prophets, with Christ Jesus himself as the cornerstone. [40]

Two contrasting approaches to creation in the Christian tradition

In preparing to die well, we will be influenced by our whole approach to life and faith. The Christian tradition itself has several approaches that have been influential in developing our contemporary theological position. However, the one thing each of these major approaches shares is that the quality of life as lived day by day is a matter of the utmost importance. The traditions may usefully, though incompletely, be classified into two theological styles: each has been influential in forming the Christian approach to life and our experience of evil and sin whose wages are death. Though it can be a little misleading to do so, the first has been associated with Augustine of Hippo, the second with Irenaeus. [41]

Augustine described humankind as having been born, as perfect creatures, into a world of absolute delight in which all was naturally divine, suffused with God's living presence. Despite this, for no intelligible reason beyond sheer selfish ingratitude, fear and greed, men and women despised their environment and sought to take possession of everything they could grasp for their own private purposes. They thus denied the true nature of God's world, frustrated the will of God for the whole creation, and by their destructive behaviour created a make-believe world of their own, in which there was no God. This self-fulfilling attitude brought eternal death upon the human race.

However, the unreality of their pretend world could not endure the reality of God's loving presence. The suffering and despair they endured when they lost the ability to enjoy the delightful environment into which they had been born were just punishments for their sin. Nevertheless, notwithstanding their 'possession' by the unreal powers of evil (anthropomorphized in the tradition as Satan) and their placing of themselves outside the reach of their own natural resources, humankind in principle still lay within the real, unvanquished power of God's love. Moreover, it was still God's nature and therefore God's will to save humankind from the hell of ignorance and the illusory power of evil possession. The creation, as the continuing work of God, remained in the most powerful sense good. God therefore sent his Son, whom we call Jesus Christ, and by whose death and resurrection God defeated the power of evil and revealed to a faithless world the continuing power and love of God. Belief in Christ as God's sacrifice for human sin, commitment of oneself to serve him, obedience to God's commands, and the acceptance of the authority of the Church, which Christ had instituted, were the means by which every human person could be saved.

There have been many responses to this 'Augustinian' tradition, many of them associated with fear of God's judgement and the desire to find a religious authority on which to place full reliance for salvation, whether that be the Bible or the Church. Ecclesiastical authority in every denomination, from Roman Catholicism, through Anglicanism, to Protestantism, Methodism and the Free Churches has, in support of false claims, often misleadingly and mistakenly exploited an Augustinian view. It has often stimulated a dour attitude to life and a fixed view of revelation such that it has diminished the delight that we should have at our increasing knowledge and our capacity to make sense of the world. Such mistaken attitudes on the part of these ecclesiastical authorities have, as many critics have asserted, led them from time to time to behave in ways that have enslaved the consciences of believers and led them to the miserable captivity of very limited lives. Legalism flowing from fear has flourished in institutional religion, rather than the love, which is actually at the heart of all things in this divinely natural world that God is in process of creating.

Two examples must suffice out of many that could be adduced.

Charles Davis notoriously resigned from the Catholic Church in 1967 because he believed that the bureaucratic and, as he understood it, unintelligent, unloving and indifferent authority of the Church was suffocating him.[42] Philip Pullman has dealt with his own experience of the Christian Church most beautifully and vividly in a trilogy of books. He works out what he believes will be the thrilling consequences for all human life when and if, at last, it is liberated from the lying power of the churches which with cynical exploitation of the human fear of death have imposed a miserable regime on humanity for their own greedy purposes. In his opinion, the Christian Church has systematically stultified human intellectual aspiration, denied the value of moral freedom, removed the human capacity to take delight without guilt in the beauty of the world around us, and subverted those institutions that might otherwise have encouraged human maturity.[43] There is too much truth in this view for comfort.

St Irenaeus, however, while accepting some of the points of St Augustine, held a contrary view. He has been somewhat less influential until recently perhaps because his views are less easily domesticated within a closed ecclesiastical authoritarianism. God, he believed, had graciously created humankind with the opportunity for eternal life in a delightful world intended precisely to encourage loving progress towards knowledge, truth and God. It would, of course, require careful attention and moral sensitivity if each person were to make the necessary progress. The courage, discipline, insight, affection, loyalty and intelligence demanded were an integral part of the enterprise. However, inexperience, immaturity and moral ineptitude, had led humankind from time to time to give up hope and to take wrong directions, leaving them lost in a confusing world of failure and often misery. Human experience of life and the world of creation was not all bad, however; indeed, part of the confusion came about from the fact that while their experience offered both good and evil, they did not always know what to do for the best. Fear of failure and of death, and the need to protect themselves from suffering, often led to self-regarding action, whereas their long-term spiritual maturity depended upon self-realization through other-regarding behaviour, moral enquiry and intellectual development.

The views I have associated with the name of St Irenaeus have produced a contrary set of criticisms that are almost as powerful. The objections of Christian conservative believers have much in common, interestingly, with those offered by many unbelievers. They both agree that any deviation from statements which follow the traditional position usually associated with Christian belief is 'not Christian really'. The traditional position may be identified with a rattle bag of doctrinal statements extracted from the Church's history. 'God created the world in six days.' 'Eve was constructed out of Adam's rib.' 'The walls of Jericho fell down when priests blew their trumpets.' 'St Paul wrote all the Epistles attributed to him.' One could go on. All such accusations assume that theological enquiry is the one and only form of human enquiry that is immune from criticism and development, fixed like 'Blackpool' through a stick of rock. It is as if the worlds of science, literary criticism, history, sociology, the creative arts, for example, despite their obvious influence upon the way human beings think of themselves, live with one another and treat the world, somehow had nothing to say about the meaning of life and the way we consider our relationship with God.

Anyone holding such a position, they seem to think, should be honest and declare himself or herself to be an unbeliever. Marian Evans, for example, when she did come to think that traditional formulations of the faith were unbelievable, recognized her unbelief and became the honest George Eliot. They each refer to the beliefs of liberals as wishy-washy, ill-defined and inconsistent with the Faith. Conservative Christians often add to the accusations they lay at the door of liberals that they hold unreasonably optimistic views on human nature and therefore suffer from hubris. They are 'puffed up' by their failure to recognize the seriousness of sin.

These brief outlines of St Augustine and St Irenaeus are incomplete and inadequate as accounts of the theological positions of either of them. Indeed, the contrast of their views is perhaps exaggerated, but they represent styles of Christian living that have greatly influenced the development of the tradition and many of the criticisms which are currently made of it. Is the faithful Christian constrained to believe certain doctrines whatever the evidence, or is one free to explore the tradition in the light of contemporary reflection? It is clear which view I take. But whatever your position on these two contrasting points of view, there is still the matter of death and how we should prepare for it so that we die well. For the Christian especially, but for everybody in fact, this is or should be a very important question. What image do you have in your mind? For the Christian, life is more than a preparation for death, though a human life that does not take account of its mortality will be an incomplete life.

Learning to die well

One can understand how, if one takes the position I have attached to the name of St Augustine as the absolute truth, human life could be lived in fear of eternal damnation, justly condemned for the rejection by the human race and by oneself of God and the impossible pursuit of a cogent and sensible life despite one's sin. Actually this is a mistake: life is not a series of tests for faith, conducted in a vale of tears, in preparation for an examination before God the Father. One may hope that the results may be weighted in one's favour because of the work and sacrifice of Jesus Christ on the cross, but one can never be sure. I say that this is a mistake, though my opinion would be widely contested. It all depends whether one believes in hell, and, if one does, what one believes about it.

Pope Benedict XVI certainly appears to believe in hell: he recently reminded Catholics in a Roman parish of the eternal existence of hell. Indeed, he assured his congregation that 'Jesus came to tell us that he wants all of us in Paradise and that hell – which few speak of in our times – exists and is eternal for those who close themselves from his love.'[44] This statement received wide press coverage and was interpreted by some as confirming their worst fears of his undeveloped conservatism. However, it is entirely consistent with the, to my mind, more reasonable view that Jesus declared hell to be an eternal *possibility* for a person who continued throughout life to reject the love of God. Jesus did not assert that there would, in the end, be anybody who actually chose to resist God; but nevertheless the freedom for someone to do so was something that God was willing to die to preserve. It is, as it were, a precondition of the contrary freedom inherent in the human condition, the freedom to identify oneself with God in Christ and to work for the freedom of all things. There were, significantly, two criminals crucified with Jesus. One could argue that their contrasting words, confirmed the ultimate reality of both heaven and hell. The one condemned himself, the other confessed and was affirmed by Jesus.

Of course, there were followers of Jesus – there still are – and indeed some theologians who claimed and continue to claim hell to be a real place of eternal punishment. However, the Jews and early Christians were no foreigners to metaphor and its importance in making a point. For example, a reference to hell in the context of the seriousness with which questions of life and death should be faced is entirely consistent with the Jewish tradition of Gehenna – the Valley of Hinnom, an actual place located to the south and south-west of Jerusalem long associated with human sacrifice and therefore a place for those totally rejected through their evil ways. If you don't wake up to the richness of life's opportunities you might as well be dead!

It would be unhelpful therefore to reject totally the imagery implicit in the Augustinian pattern of faith, but quite wrong to accept it as the literal framework within which human life had to be lived and its outcome endured. The person who rejects the divinely natural dimension of God's creation sees things in the dark and limits the range of his potential achievements to what he can bring within his own control. In principle, this is very little. Eventually he will become isolated in his own fears and jealousies, closed to anyone or anything else, which is exactly what some theologians have suggested hell is: not a place but a state of mind, a condition of the soul in which one does not find any 'others' to link with.[45] Indeed, this becomes apparent to us in the course of an ordinary human life as we emerge from adolescence to adult maturity and begin to experience the freedom for self-knowledge that comes from giving oneself to the other in friendship, affection and love.

The Irenaean perspective is not wholly different in its purpose, which is to account for the actual condition in which human beings find themselves and propose ways forward. However, whereas Augustine explains the parlous human situation as the just punishment for sin, Irenaeus believes that the human condition comes about from the failure of human beings to grasp the opportunities for maturation that God places before humankind. Perhaps this is because they doubt their own abilities and, as Paul says, 'fall short of the glory of God' by settling for something less than the wholeness, indeed the holiness, which they are promised.[46]

From either perspective, it is clear that life for each human being amounts to something which is present, something which is going on at the present moment: it is not simply governed by the attitude of the believer to the end of life in death. Learning to die well is a matter of dying with the hope of salvation, and this stems from learning how, day by day, to live well. It is something to do with learning to appreciate what one has, who one is, to make the most of it, and to keep in mind that what one appreciates now will be of eternal significance. It is not of course always easy to do this, but it can be done.

Many things militate against giving one's attention to the present. Life may be consumed with anxiety for the future. The condition of the environment, climate change, the price of fuel, the threat of a shortage of water, terrorism, the decline of study of ancient history, the anti-intellectualism of most public debate – almost anything can cause anxiety. Some things one may be able to do something about. I could turn the heating down and wear an extra jersey; I could walk rather than use the car; I could wake up to the fact that money is not the only reason for living, and take pleasure in my friends. I could try to show others the value of studying ancient history. But when I've done that, instead of succumbing to the despair brought on by my state of anxiety, perhaps I would be better employed getting down to the task of reading more of the original texts in order to demonstrate the unique stimulus which comes from studying a period of history where most people can become familiar with most of the evidence.

Wracked with fear of something beyond my immediate influence, undermined by envy of another's success or angered by the frustrating attitude implicit in some bureaucrat's ignorant behaviour, I may lose the capacity to pay attention to the aspects of life within my grasp which will nourish my sense of self and enable me properly to work with others to open up future possibilities. This process means that I become less open to the worlds of experience promised to me by the mere fact of my birth.

Baptizatus sum: I have been baptized

The daily freshness of life for the Christian is instantiated in baptism, which Paul describes as 'dying and rising with Christ'.[47] The Christian in baptism shares in the wholeness of God's love for the world as presented in Christ, the Living Word. It is important to understand both the public and interior aspect of baptism signified in the sacramental action by 'water and the Spirit' if we are to come to terms with life's opportunities, as offered by God in Christ through the Spirit. It is worth underlining the fact that baptism is unconditional and is so regarded by all the major Christian denominations. It is true that in the event that there is doubt whether a person is baptized, the Roman Catholic and Anglican Churches baptize 'again' but then only conditionally. It is in principle understood by all traditions that baptism is a once-and-for-all event: as Luther said, '*Baptizatus sum*: I have been baptized![48] That's it; one either is baptized or one is not!

To be baptized is both an event and a state of life in the sense that having been baptized one is 'a baptized person' for ever. The priority and vitality of baptism is apparent because a priest or minister usually celebrates the sacrament, though not even this is essential. *In extremis* a member of the laity (who may or may not even be a Christian) perhaps a nurse in the case of a sick child, or a travelling companion in the event of an accident, may perform the rite. What does matter is the form of the words, 'Michael John, I baptize you in the name of the Father and of the Son and of the Holy Spirit', and the use of water, preferably running water if it is available. But what then does baptism signify?

Time was when most Christians believed that without baptism one was condemned to hell or at best limbo. The reasoning was that unbaptized persons were excluded from eternal happiness perhaps because even the youngest children shared in original sin even if their lives were so short that they could hardly have actually sinned. This teaching was never part of the official teaching of the magisterium of the Catholic Church, and while even the Second Vatican Council still encourages the urgent baptism of newly born children, the point is to bear witness to the inclusion of even the least of one of these children within the grace of God's love. But baptism is not a *sine qua non* of salvation: it is an outward and visible sign of the inner grace that declares that each person lives both in the presence of the divine and is rooted in the physical world of flesh and blood. To become oneself, therefore, and to fulfil the promises of God confirmed in the dying and rising of Christ, which are affirmed in baptism for every person, a person is committed to finding their place within their first communities of family and faith and developing relationships with all the communities open to them.

The foundational community is the community of faith. If one does not grow in familiarity with that community, one will lack the insights that illuminate one's life with divine grace. The consequence will be an inclination to settle into a world based upon the assumption that life is to be lived in the extremely important but essentially two-dimensional world of mere human interaction first instantiated in the family. The community of faith, the Church, the Body of Christ, into which one has been baptized, is no private world; it is not a world into which one has withdrawn from the real world, it is the real world in which one has life, from which one withdraws at peril. The conversation of God with the Church, and of the Church with the world, is all-inclusive. Thus, to be a baptized person commits one to giving attention to the world in its wholeness, finding one's way about as many of the worlds that are potentially open to one as is possible, and to the business of taking a place in as many of the communities which are open to one as is reasonable.

What does this mean for the business of learning to live well day by day, and therefore for the analogously important business of learning to die well? First, one grows into one's family. As I first find my own body and learn to distinguish between what is here – my toes – and what is 'there' – the blanket – I begin to become aware of the power of speech. 'Talking' is something we do from the very beginning of life. It does not focus exclusively upon the limited purposes of securing food, drink, warmth and comfort, important though these are; there is the wider purpose of finding oneself, of getting oneself understood, of establishing relationships, of trying to understand one's world, to find one's way about, to make sense of it and to enjoy oneself.

In order to do this we graduate from the informal environment of learning where play was our personal experiment with the whole world of scholarship and meaning, to the more organized world where we formally enter into the 'conversation between the generations' in order to share 'experience and its modes'.[49] Our attempts to come to terms with who we are, what we are capable of and what are the limits of our powers have taken many forms. The physical sciences, mathematics, the social sciences, together with the technical developments that they have spawned, are the most prominent influences on current changes in human self-understanding. Yet the grammar, vocabulary and syntax of our natural languages and the difficulties of translation, are all influential. But if we do not pay attention to historical enquiry, philosophical reflection, ethical insight and theological enquiry, we shall lose touch with our inheritance and be lost in a confusing maze of contradictory paths leading nowhere except to irrational conflict, prejudice, intolerance and renewed attempts to build private worlds of meaning – personal, social, national, international, regional, religious and generational.

In this exciting framework, which is in principle life-affirming because of all the opportunities it places before us, there is the threat of dissolution, destruction and death. It is apparent to everyone that the world is beyond us in the sense that we cannot control it all and render it subject to our own wills. It is not only beyond our power to subject another to our will. We know this only too well, but unless we keep it in the forefront of our minds, we shall lose all perspective on the present in order to prepare for a dark future.

Learning to live well, in society, with ourselves and with one another, it is necessary to keep in mind the openness of our understanding, the openness of the love which lies at the heart of all human experience, and the divine nature which *in fact* we do have, and can learn to rely on. By our formation in the faith which is open to us, we will not come completely to understand all things, but we will be able increasingly to *embody* the truth which we declare. The Church's task, its role and nature as the Body of Christ in which we share, is to 'talk the talk and live the life'.

If we learn to do that, we shall live well day by day, and therefore have learned to die well – day by day. As de Caussade wrote, 'The most solid preparation for death is that which we make every day, by a regular life, a spirit of recollection, of annihilation, of abnegation, patience, charity and union with our Lord.'[50]

3

The Naturalness of It All

There is nothing unnatural about any aspect of human life, especially when one includes death and the fear of death. To make such a claim is, of course, unilluminating in itself and solves no problems because it all depends what one means by 'natural'.

It would be foolish to assume, *tout court*, that determining the meaning of a word will resolve seriously difficult conceptual and practical questions. But careful attention to a word's meaning can help to clear the decks for further exploratory work. Take for example the use of the word 'natural' when applied to the sciences. Some regard the results of enquiry by means of methods developed in the '*natural* sciences' to cover all matters that can be regarded as knowledge in any useful sense. By 'natural' when applied to the sciences, they mean such enquiries as depend for their significance upon data provided in principle by the five senses, organized according to the agreed methods of scientific enquiry. Indeed, there are those who go beyond this and regard people who hold any contrary view as simpletons. How can they be argued with when their belief is that there is supernatural knowledge that by definition is outside the range of normal conversation? However, many question this approach and I would agree with them.

Natural and supernatural: the openness of all human enquiry

So what about the supernatural? Supernatural knowledge – if there is such a thing – is not so much non-natural, as most deeply natural. It might be said that it reveals what is most revealingly natural about the natural: it uncovers the implicit structures that are beyond immediate empirical investigation. After all, the implicit assumption that other forms of enquiry – and there are many – are somehow 'unnatural' must be nonsense: there can be no form of enquiry known to humankind that is 'unnatural'. So if we are to define knowledge as that offered exclusively through the natural sciences, then we had better be clear that 'natural science' also covers all those other dimensions of enquiry to which we are committed and which have been found revealing for human self-understanding. These include, among many others, philosophy, the social sciences, history, theology, economics, psychology, the arts, architecture, garden design, and even perhaps especially, metaphysics.

We should simplify things for ourselves if we simply regarded the 'natural' sciences as special, intriguing and valuable ways of enquiring about our experience, but it is not an all-inclusive term since it does not cover all sensible learning. There is more to life than what is covered, for example, by physics, chemistry, cosmology, biochemistry and neurophysiology. Personally, I like the approach of Hilary Putnam, the Princeton philosopher, though the gamut of intelligent human enquiry open to us in our human condition is, in my opinion, actually even wider than perhaps he believes to be legitimate.

Putnam began his career thinking about the nature of mathematics and scientific enquiry. He has latterly ranged more broadly but with equal sharpness when reflecting upon our contemporary intellectual, moral and cultural predicament. In a recent book, he writes:

I think that Aristotle was profoundly right in holding that ethics is concerned with how to live and with human happiness, and also profoundly right in holding that this sort of *knowledge* (practical knowledge) is different from theoretical knowledge. A view of knowledge that acknowledges that the sphere of knowledge is wider that the sphere of 'science' seems to me to be a cultural necessity if we are to arrive at a sane and human view of ourselves *or* of science.[51]

There are two points here that necessarily broaden our understanding of what it means to be human and how we think about our knowledge. There is first the matter of moral behaviour. How should we live our lives? This has much to do, as Aristotle argued, with what we believe about human nature, the quality of happiness and the nature of virtue. Putnam suggests that there are many aspects of life, for example wine-making, brilliant architecture and a successful marriage, which are not capable of systematic analysis in terms of a conventional approach to the natural sciences. Each activity certainly requires technical knowledge, the development of skills and attention to detail, but also an innate '*Je ne sais quoi*' beyond precise description. However, they are all perfectly natural. But if that is so, how much more is this the case when we consider the infinitely more complex and variable patterns of intelligent enquiry concerned with 'learning to live well' and – as I would want to add – dying well too!

Socrates, as reported by Plato, understood this perfectly well. Living and dying are both things that we do. They raise practical questions; in the certain knowledge of death there were things to be resolved. Thus Socrates' last words are reputed to have been, 'Crito, we owe a cock to Aesculapius; pay it, therefore, do not neglect it.'[52] But it also raised other sorts of questions that did not succumb to immediate practical or even scientific solutions. And these merited further consideration, as Socrates declares in the final words of his Apology. 'Now it is time that we were going, I to die and you to live, but which of us has the happiest prospect is unknown to anyone but God.'[53]

'Yet,' Putnam suggests, 'the fact that one cannot reduce living well to a science does not mean that reflecting on how to live well is not a rational enterprise, or that there cannot be any objective knowledge about it.'[54] To think, for example, that moral reflection can be effectively done by attention to the facts of the case without the use of the imagination is simply wrong. And let's put aside for the moment the very complex question concerning what the facts are that are relevant in a particular case: other aspects of our life together inform our capacity for good moral judgement. Indeed, as Putnam goes on to argue, there is a crucial role for the imagination in constructive ethical reflection that is largely undervalued or ignored by the philosophical tradition, but deprived of the imagination ethical reflection would be in principle impossible. The practical knowledge gained through the use of the imagination is presented to our minds principally through the arts – drama, film, fiction, painting, music, sculpture and the like. To learn to 'read' novels is to open worlds of experience to us, which we can enter through the imagination and through which we can grow to a more sensitive maturity. This is reflected in the languages and styles of criticism that we have developed in which to express, discuss, evaluate and share insights into our human nature. These are of profound importance; through them we gain knowledge that we interiorize through conversation. It is natural to be interested in another's perspective, and to want to gain from absorbing their experience in order to enhance our capacity for sound judgement. What one gains from such exercise of the imagination, moreover, is properly regarded as knowledge.

The second point is that our consideration of the virtuous life will include an explicit, or more likely implicit but nevertheless real because influential, understanding of what it is to be human. We form in the light of our total experience a view of 'human nature'; but that raises a significant question. Is there such a thing as human nature existing in itself with qualities and limitations with which we have to work? If so, what are those qualities and limitations? How do we work with them in order to bring to fruition our real natures? Perhaps there are no necessary characteristics of human nature, and the attempt to uncover them is simply illusory. Is our humanity actually the accidental product of the interaction of nature and nurture and, therefore, within very broad limits, infinitely malleable? Can we become whatever we choose to be within the limits of mortality? In attempting to answer these questions about our human nature, there is no area of public discussion that is irrelevant. Most particularly, it must never be forgotten that the many religions give form and intellectual space to what it is to be human, to its essential nature and how it has and will flourish. Their embodiment in ways of life that naturally include both matters of worship and ritual, together with behaviour that is consistent with them, is a significant influence upon human flourishing. Far from being an aspect of life that is dying the death of disbelief, our everyday experience confirms their living influence.

Practical concerns

Questions about the nature of human knowledge, and whether there is such a thing as human nature, are indeed very practical concerns that influence our behaviour. They are not the only aspects of life that matter to humankind and define our self-understanding. Clive Bell provocatively argued that civilization and therefore high culture depended upon the acquisition of sufficient wealth to provide for a leisured elite.[55] I rather agree with this, yet it would be idle to suggest that only the leisured classes are in a position to puzzle about life, its meaning and purpose. We all quite naturally find ourselves caught up in the ordinary business of living. Getting and spending, care for the well-being of our families, conflicts arising at work, anxiety in the face of disease, the pressures of travel and the cost of living can take up all our time if we allow them too. Indeed, there are those upon whom the demands are such that they cannot think about anything else. The sufferings of some people – too many! – mean that those of us who live in more lively and privileged surroundings can hardly imagine how they could ever think in a larger and more fulfilling perspective. The media are full of images that outrage and humiliate decent sensibilities. When we catch a glimpse of what is going on when presented in text, film or photograph it is not so much the fact of death itself that arouses our ire and anxiety, it is the evidence on a daily basis of the sheer cruelty, bestiality and terror of which humankind is capable. Yet that is not the only perspective that we have on the human situation. Even in the deepest crisis, the most demanding pressure, one can think and question: it is natural to do so. We are not plunged irretrievably and inevitably into a maelstrom of repetitive senselessness; there is still the hope of meaning that is provided for by the fact of death.

It was Heidegger, the great German philosopher of the twentieth century, who commented on the 'ordinary average everydayness' of being caught up in the ordinary affairs of human life.[56] He regarded such an existence as meaningless: as we might say colloquially, when thought of from this point of view, life is just one damn thing after another! Heidegger saw death, on the other hand, as offering the opportunity for a transformation of life because it provided what he called *Dasein* (the 'Being-there' of life) with the fact of its ending such that it defined the 'Being-as-a-whole' of the entity which exists. 'The entity which exists' is the person each of us is, you and I. Each of us, because of death, owns a life; for 'my' life can be lived by nobody else while my life exists or indeed after my death. Each of us has a potential and real totality of experience because there is no eternally continuing coming-to-be for us. The facticity of death, which gives the reality of wholeness to a life, therefore provides for each individual life the necessary opportunity for responsibility if it is to have meaning. What is more, it is a creative meaning because, as life is lived and choices are made, there is an impact upon both the past and the future. The meaning of a life is not a given, it is not predetermined; it is something to which we contribute or even make for ourselves. In this lies hope, but a hope that must be grasped if it is to have any present significance.

There is another point to add here which, I think, helps us to understand what we mean when we talk of 'the present'. Edmund Husserl, who much influenced Heidegger, seems to have regarded the literal present as a fiction – a moment that does not really exist except in relation to the past and the future. He referred to human consciousness as having a real existence in what he referred to as 'an extended present', for being a self-conscious self is to be conscious (in however limited a degree), with a past and a future for both of which we can become responsible because of the capacity to remember, reflect, plan, intend, choose and determine which is innate in every human person.[57]

In this space there lies human freedom which, of course, one may use well or irresponsibly. An event acquires shape and takes its meaning over time; we people the future with our hopes and fears, and take responsibility for it, as far as we can, by doing what we can to bring the best to fruition.

Deceptive aspirations

But this can be hard; regret at failure and guilt at outcomes prey upon our minds. The anxieties generated by the uncertainties of choice have led people to entertain a large number of strategies by means of which to cope. Ernst Bloch, for example, had challenging experiences on which to base his personal exercise of his human freedom. A Marxist philosopher, he kept his powder dry by escaping from an oppressive Nazism to America, returning after the war to live in what he hoped would be the revolutionary freedom of the German Democratic Republic. But political reaction to his unorthodox ideas led him to relocate yet again to Western Germany. He reflected on the human condition in an engrossing trilogy, *The Principle of Hope*, where he reviewed some of the ways proposed and pursued over the course of human history to find a secure foundation in order to avoid yet more frustration and ignorant behaviour.[58] Surely there must be some basis for human action on which we can rely without fear! The perspective he opens up is huge, ranging from daydreaming, ambitious metaphors and allegories, to utopias of great diversity, technological, geographical, economic and the like. We indulge many of them today in the light of our false hopes for enduring personal happiness. We shall, we believe, be better off if we relocate, change our partner, extend our house, win the lottery, or even change the world! Not all of these are irrelevant; some will inspire, encourage maturity and bring new opportunity. But to be significant they all require a time-frame, an explicit set of dimensions if they are to be meaningful. Death has to be an assumption built in to every enterprise and every life.

The hopes which Bloch gives us are all 'natural' responses to the very natural *fear* of death that life's experiences can otherwise promote: life without meaning is intolerable. Meaninglessness, pointlessness are far more awful than death itself. No wonder we try to escape them by imaginative enterprise! But they are found, paradoxically, in all utopias where we try to command the future and determine it after our own image. If we can produce arguments which purport persuasively to establish beyond question the underlying inevitabilities on which our utopia is based, so much the better. Perhaps then we can persuade ourselves that we have not only the right but also the duty to bring others to accept our point of view. Totalitarianisms and fundamentalisms of all kinds share this awful illusion. In accepting them we succumb to a death wish, which is inevitably successful. In looking to escape death by embracing an uncriticizable and undevelopable utopianism, we choose to die.

Grasping after transcendence: the divine dimension

Intriguingly, Bloch was profoundly aware of this. Hence, despite his atheism, he grasped after a sense of self-transcendence that was to be found in the religious traditions, most especially in Christianity. It was a self-transcendence that was dynamic and developmental, characterized by meliorism, not utopian finalities. Hence he has influenced theology, especially Jürgen Moltmann, for theology makes room for the partnership of God and humankind that is characterized by the depths of personal relationship and maturity.[59] Moltmann recognized that death was a necessary condition of all *human* life, because it revealed the impossibility of building utopia and the reality of the ever-present grace of God to encourage life.

For the Christian tradition, given the belief that creation in all its dimensions owes its origin and nature to God, a conversation between all forms of enquiry and the information divulged through their successful pursuit is a natural assumption, especially a conversation between the sciences and theology. Thomas Torrance entitled his Hewitt Lectures, *Theological Science*; he has a point.[60] However, it is a *theological* science, not a *natural* science, notwithstanding the fact that I want to argue that both are natural. Both are concerned with the nature of our human being. Theology does not deny anything that has been established on the basis of the natural sciences, but claims that a true account of our human nature depends upon the placing of it, and all creation, within the realm of a reality that is more completely describable in theological terms. Moreover, science, if it is sensibly grounded in human experience, will have room for the contribution of such dynamic reflection on meaning and purpose as Putnam underlined.

Christian theology, its interpretation in the disciplines of the spiritual life and the thinking about authority in the historical churches, has often dwelt upon the notion of the fear of the Lord. When it has been intelligently discussed it has been in association with God's justice and what that might mean in relation to the fundamental appreciation of God as loving and all-powerful. It is perfectly natural to be torn between a desire for God as the ground of all that is affectionate and delightful, and a fear of God the rightful deliverer of justice, which we are only too well aware we deserve. To hold them together so as to release us from our fears into the peaceful, healing presence of God our Father, demands a lifetime of intelligent reflection and emotional coherence.

It is far from easy. The Christian churches have tried to deal with the matter theologically in several ways. Canon Law, conceived in terms of pastoral ecclesiology, is one way of approaching it. Looked at in this way, the purpose of Canon Law is to support an individual's search for truth, love and faith in the face of failure, not to determine punishment or to exact penalties. All too frequently, however, the churches in their respective approaches have allowed their ministers to interpret the precepts of Canon Law as a means of justifying their impersonal decisions in personal affairs in support of a weak church or an insecure clergy person. So employed, Canon Law, which was always intended to bring life, obscures God's living presence and brings death.

49

Purgatory is another approach that has been developed to help us hold together God's love and God's justice. It is a place and way of life for those who are not condemned to hell but who suffer under God's justice because they are not free from sin. But since they long to be free and to know God's love for them and his longing intention to welcome them into his presence in due course, they are, as it were, *en route* for a closer walk with God. God's love and justice are satisfied. I note with some interest, however, that Pope Benedict has allowed a review of the doctrine because, in the minds of some theologians and even more Christians, it seems to give greater weight to God's justice than to God's love. It is almost as if there is a quota of satisfaction required for each sin, even those unconfessed venial sins. But surely that is to fail to do justice to the God revealed in Christ, whose commitment of God's self to the other – the Creation – makes up for all that is lacking so that he or she can recognize God for who God is. Certainly one may hope so – and hope in Christ is the basis of an understanding of a doctrine of Purgatory. There are grounds to believe that continuing reflection on the nature of God in the light of Christ will further clarify and illuminate the reality of God's love.

Most recently the Pope has approved the recommendation of the Vatican Theological Commission to remove the concept of limbo from Roman Catholic teaching.[61] Augustine taught that unbaptized children went to hell; the justification was that while they may not have sinned, they still shared the human consequences of original sin. But the commonsensical response to this is that such a judgement is intolerable. Some amelioration took place as this thought gradually sunk in, so that limbo became a place where there was no actual suffering, but where also there was no appreciation of the vision of God. Holding together God's justice and God's love in creative tension is undoubtedly difficult, but it can be done: it depends upon appreciating 'the naturalness of it all' within a framework which embraces God and Creation.

Tillich writes of the mystical *a priori*, by which he is usually taken to mean the indefinable wholeness of things that is implicitly given in philosophical and theological enquiry. The wholeness of things is never glimpsed, let alone seen and understood; but without a realization that there is a 'wholeness of things' that lies behind and within every intelligent appreciation of a particular aspect of it, there could be no meaning. Tillich referred to this reality as God, the Ground of our Being. Rahner approached the matter in a different way. Given that God is both Creator and Redeemer of his world, he argued that there could be no such thing as 'ungraced nature'. In creating, God was personally committed: God gave God's self to the world. The world is not therefore an aspect of God, nor some thing independent of God that God had entered or taken over; it was and is a natural world capable of assuming everything that is divine, without damage to God's own nature or the nature of creation. The wholeness of things, the mystical *a priori* that is vouchsafed in every experience, is incompletely conceived unless the attempt to understand it and respond to it includes God, Father, Son and Holy Spirit. In the most profound sense, *all* human experience is *naturally* both experience of God and of the world.

Revelation and the Beatific Vision

What then of revelation? Revelation, insofar as we can make sense of the term at all, is the constant uncovering of what is really natural and implicit within our experience that declares its true nature; it is not the intrusion of something from outside into our natural world. Revelation and reason cohere in our search for God; their apparent conflict from time to time is the stimulus to enquiry and understanding to which we are committed if we are to grow in faith. Most certainly the idea that a doctrine of revelation carries with it any notion of certainty is wholly erroneous![62] Pseudo-Dionysius was right when he argued that conceptually we might accept that ontologically revelation is prior to reason, as God is prior to the world he created. However, God may be known in and through any created thing; even if that knowledge takes us only a short way towards God, it is God's self that we imperfectly intuit. The insight of Pseudo-Dionysius is a constant corrective to those who would seek to domesticate God in man-made systems of doctrine or insist that they and they alone have the true way to encounter him.[63]

It is for this reason that Christians have the potential to glimpse the Beatific Vision. Human creatureliness includes the possibility of holiness, of sharing in the divine, or being swept up into the whole community of God's Trinitarian being. Abbot Marmion, the distinguished Benedictine writer on spirituality, wrote:

> Holiness, in man, is only possible according to the Divine Plan: to know this plan, to adapt oneself to it is the whole substance of holiness. This plan consists in calling the human creature to participate, by the grace of supernatural adoption, in God's own eternal life.[64]

'Divine plan' can be a very misleading term, as also can the term 'supernatural', as we have seen. But if we take them to refer to the vital necessity for human flourishing of appreciating that God's loving 'strategy' is to make a world in which it is possible for God to be known and for the world to know God, it makes good sense. God's strategy is to *be here* in the world so that there is a personal invitation inherent in every human person to become a member, a part of the body of Christ.

The Venerable Bede grasps after much the same point but uses it to underline the possibility of effective prayer. He writes in one of the homilies:

> 'Be holy for I the Lord your God am holy (Lev. 19.2).' Now this is the image of God in which we were fashioned in the first human being, so that we might be holy for ever by participation in the divine holiness. Hence the psalmist's words, 'You have set upon us the light of your countenance, O Lord' (Ps. 4.7). But because humanity lost this light of the divine countenance by sinning, it pleased God to assume the condition of a human countenance by being born in the flesh, so that thereby he might teach us that we should be reborn in the spirit; and

it pleased him to appear in the likeness of sinful flesh yet without sin, so that he might cleanse us from every sin and reform in us the clarity of his image.[65]

The language is difficult for us, but implicitly he is arguing that the natural world for human beings is this one, which involves both the human and the divine. To describe our experience in either human or divine terms, as if one language could precisely cover all our experience, is simply wrong. What is more, God has seen to it that despite our deserts, God is present to us so that we can still dwell in his presence for ever, if only we will understand that it is so, and desire it for ourselves. Therefore we can have confidence that when we address God, God hears us.

Implicit in this is an understanding that for humankind there is always the mysterious possibility of the Beatific Vision – the transforming, gracious because unsought and undeserved, society of the Divine. It can be anticipated in this life though never completely known and certainly not in such a way as to deny God's essential incomprehensibility. Indeed, to deny humankind's openness to the Beatific Vision would be to deny the natural relationship of God and God's world. Sadly there are those who believe that the Beatific Vision can be gained instantaneously and without effort and that having so gained it they are somehow privileged above all others. Of course, they are grievously wrong; it cannot be so gained.

It is hard to produce analogies and harder still to justify them. But let me try. We will all have friends, members of the family, whom we know very well and in whose company we take great delight. Their presence renews us, enlivens us and brings us joy. We would be mistaken, however, if we were to claim that we knew them utterly. We know, on the other hand, that when we are with such a friend or family member we are with a person and in a personal relationship. Just occasionally we see them anew in a light that is revelatory; our understanding of them and appreciation of their personhood gains a new depth. And we are grateful. Nevertheless, we would, I hope, never want to claim that that was all there was to it: now we know perfectly as it were, there is nothing else to know. That would be far from the truth. Indeed, if what we have learned is true, the relationship will have changed even if we do not say anything about it, because we will have been changed. Our mutual opportunities for shared creativity, our capacity to be for others, will have grown.

The Beatific Vision, the fullness of the experience of God's presence with the individual believer, is open to every person, through the grace of baptism, which, as Abbot Marmion says, contains the whole substance of the human–divine union. There is celebrated in baptism the fullness of God's presence with God's world. The idea of the Beatific Vision underlines the wholeness of things, the natural continuity of human life with the divine life.

In order to get the full picture we should take seriously the Catholic principle, 'First what is natural, second what is of grace.' We should first note that this is not a matter of the order in which they stand ontologically, as if it is somehow better to leave out what is natural if one can. Rather, it is only by appreciating the true dimensions of the natural that we can discern the graciousness of the divine presence. Second, as a matter of fact it is only by discernment of the full nature of the world of God's creation within our ordinary experience that we can begin to understand and interiorize the love of God. Third, nothing that is of grace diminishes the value of what is open to us in everyday life. Indeed, it gives it a sparkle and resonance that illuminates God's love. Moreover, nothing is excluded from this, including the completeness that is offered to us in death. To accept death as defining our natural life is to declare the absolute reality of God's gracious presence in everything that pertains to human well-being. We do indeed die, as we have lived, in the presence of God, Father, Son and Holy Spirit.

The Incarnation is the doctrine that makes sense of the naturalness of God's presence with humankind in God's good creation. In determining that God would take the first step and actually create, God understood that there would be a risk. If God was willing to take that risk, God understood, moreover, that there was no other person to take that risk but God's self. God took that risk. One might ask whether it is reasonable to talk in this anthropomorphic way: I think it must be, in virtue of the naturalness of the whole created order and the powerful mutuality of the Divine and the human. Analogy, as Aquinas profoundly understood, is the only route open to us. We have some knowledge of risk in every human relationship – parent and child, husband and wife, friend and neighbour; yet if we are unwilling to take that risk, we deny our humanity and the possibility of its flourishing. Indeed, a person who is for clinical reasons *unable* to take that risk is ill and needs professional help and an enormous amount of affection from others who are willing and able to offer it. God, as we think of God in Trinity, is precisely open and free to give just such demanding love, and was willing to do so. There is no possibility that such love *ends* in death, since death is also a part of the naturalness of life that is within the imaginative affection of the divine–human encounter.

The significant words to keep in mind are 'perfect love casts out fear'. Since the world knows the presence of the perfection that is the love of God, such completeness cannot be denied to the whole world in all its dimensions.

Let us turn now to a consideration of death itself, what it means and how we should think of those moments when we simply give ourselves to God.

> The God and Father of our Lord Jesus Christ open all our eyes, that we may see that blessed hope to which we are called; that we may altogether glorify the only God and Jesus Christ, whom he hath sent down to us from heaven; to whom with the Father and the Holy Spirit be rendered all honour and glory to all eternity. (John Jewel, 1522–71)

And may the souls of the faithful rest in peace: Amen.

This prayer, which is usually offered in respect of those who have died in the faith, should, if we properly understand the nature of the world of God's creation, be intended for the whole Communion of Saints, among whom we all live, whether alive, dead, or still to be born.

4

Death

When I died last, and, Dear, I die
As often as from thee I go,
Though it be but an hour ago,
And lovers' hours be full of eternity.
(John Donne, 'The Legacy')

What is death?

I have from time to time heard people say of some experience that it was 'a fate worse than death'. Conventional wisdom has it that there are circumstances that justify this statement. Attitudes to death differ widely of course across the ages, in different locations and from the point of view of the religious tradition in which it is set. Even within the Christian tradition there is huge variation, but with this general statement Christians wholeheartedly agree. At least I think they should. There are fates worse than death. The reason for this is that a Christian regards death as the most personal thing that any individual does in life. And that is the point: it is something which one does in life and which involves the whole of one's self, and therefore, as I have suggested above, something for which it is important to prepare well. But in order to prepare well, one needs at least some grasp, however inadequate, of what one is preparing for.

For the end? If so, of what? For the future? If so, what future? For the Christian who accepts that a personal life is the most precious thing a human being possesses, the straightforward answer to the straightforward question is, 'A meeting, at last,

with God.' Christians believe God to be the absolute perfection
of everything that is meant by Affectionate Personal Being; in
meeting and being recognized by God, therefore, Christians will
be truly confirmed in relation to their own personhood. This
traditional Christian perspective, which sets death in the context
of life with God, is the one that I wish to examine in this chapter. It is not commonly discussed; I have to wrack my memory
in order to recall any sermon that I have heard on this topic.
The nearest I can get to it is an occasion some time between
1966 and 1973 when I was chaplain of Kingswood School, John
Wesley's foundation in Bath. I shared in a conversation with the
Chapel Committee when it wrestled with the subject of 'Life
after Death?' and invited a visiting preacher to take it as his
subject for the Sunday morning service. I wish I could remember
who it was! I expect that, unlike some visiting preachers, he will
have reckoned he had to write a new sermon!

It is also clear that in our own time many who willingly affirm
their Christian faith and want to call themselves Christians
would not entertain such an idea. 'Life after death?' they say;
'Grow up! Life after death was an early aberration of the Faith
before we understood the world properly – that is, from a scientific point of view; now that we have a better understanding, our
Christian task is to focus upon the real world. The Christian's
faith illuminates the world with divine grace and inspires human
affection for God, the world and one another, quite apart from
any perspective that might be opened up by considering life after
death.' Their view is that we have grown out of this fantasy and
should get on with our Christian lives without it.

Of course, in an important sense which we explored in the
previous chapter, they are quite right. The best, indeed the only
preparation for death, is living well in the here and now. But,
for my part, I do not understand how Christian faith can make
sense apart from such a doctrine. I would not go quite as far as
E. L. Mascall who wrote a little book to help us understand the
vast dimensions of the 'natural' world as Christians experience
it, but I do agree with him that any interpretation of the universe
as Christians experience it which fails to place God's love at the

heart of the cosmos misses the point![66] Certainly, however, for most of us because our idea of ourselves is so inadequate to our experience, we entertain an understanding of God which is 'too small', not fit for purpose![67]

We are trying to work out where humankind fits in to a world that can be explained naturally as the work of God. And once we entertain the thought that our lives make sense only because they have meaning as the creation of God's redemptive love, I find it impossible to see how God could be true to God's self and abandon us just because we have died. The Christian will not sensitively accept death unless it is set within the framework of life with God. But discussion of life *after* death is not part of the consideration of death itself. Life *after* death is not the same as death. I shall discuss the question of life after death in Chapter 6, what the words might mean for us, and how we can make sense of our Christian faith that includes, in my opinion, so clearly such doctrine. Most particularly, we shall have to look with especial attention at the implications for our understanding of the temporal conjunction 'after'.

Death and dying

For our present purpose, it is important first to make a clear and fundamental distinction between death and dying. Dying is a physical, biological process, an account of which can be given, if not completely then with reasonable accuracy, by a neurophysiologist: when brain function ceases (and we have increasingly subtle means of registering this), life has come to an end. Death, on the other hand, is a metaphysical event; it refers to the moment when a person ceases to *be*. Wittgenstein remarks, 'Death is not an event in life: we do not live to experience death.'[68] There is, of course, a sense in which this is true. Nobody has been able to report to another on his own death. However, that is not the point, and indeed it may not be exactly what Wittgenstein had in mind.

The fact that death is not 'an event in life' does not imply that it is something that just happens to one and for which one cannot prepare. One can certainly bring one's life to an end by, for example, committing suicide. Not all deaths are properly regarded as involuntary happenings. And that is the point, for, on the contrary, the Christian sees making a good death as a moment of ultimate personal responsibility, something a Christian *does* and which to that extent is within her control. What the Christian is doing at the moment of death can only be described in inadequate theological terms. Thus, perhaps, we should say, 'The Christian is placing her life into the hands of God.' As Christ said, 'My Father, if it is possible, let this cup pass from me; yet not what I want but what you want.'[69]

As Ladislaus Boros says, with regard to the process of dying:

> The essential bodily functions come to a stop. The body begins to decompose, and when that happens, the most elementary co-ordination of the various individual functions is ended. Particular tissues or whole organs can indeed be preserved intact artificially, but life as a whole has become impossible; the person has 'died'. But does that mean that he is 'dead'? The question points to a *distinction between dying and death* which is of fundamental importance to our analysis.[70]

The moment of death is when a person, certainly if that person is of Christian faith, hands himself or herself to God. As I have indicated already, I find it hard to reconcile a Christian understanding of God with the thought that death puts a person beyond God – that is, outside God's love. To hand oneself over to God is to accept the reality of the fundamental relationship that has been the ground of every person's being throughout 'life'. I realize that this raises questions about who we understand God to be and also what we mean by person, self-identity and whether there is any usefulness to be gained from our continued use of the traditional term for the personal identity in relation to God, namely, soul. I discuss the nature of self-consciousness, personal identity and the soul in Chapter 5. But there are some remarks to be made here about the way in which the Christian understands God, before we can turn our

full attention to death itself, particularly the moment of truth
that is a person's death.

The meaning of 'God'

Let me first of all say that I regret the current lack of attention to the intriguingly demanding question of God's existence.
Does God exist? As I understand it, the way in which we think
through what is involved in answering the question is of the
utmost importance for the way we live our human lives and the
way in which we believe ourselves to relate to the universe in all
its dimensions. Whether a person believes that the universe has
a creator or is merely a happenstance will influence profoundly
the way in which that person lives life. More especially it will
impact upon the way in which he treats the matter of death. It
is, of course, not a question that can be answered in the abstract;
to give it due consideration one has to have in mind a particular
conception of God and examine its significance in the light of a
lifetime's experience. Belief in God is lived out both in the way
one thinks and in the way one behaves; it involves all people, and
the way in which one believes oneself to be related to them.

So how does our Christian view of God shape our understanding of life and death? How do we talk about God and God's
relationship with the world, and humankind in particular? Let's
begin with God as God is in God's self. God exists in his aseity.
This useful word has slipped out of usage – if indeed it was ever
a common part of everyday conversation! But it is an illuminating concept. What the term implies is that God owes God's
existence and nature to God's self. Nothing and no one has any
power over God: as we might say, 'God Is Who God Is And Not
Another Person.' This is the God who out of the generosity of
God's own gracious will determined to bring a world into existence which could *be* in God's image, and enjoy the delight of the
triune God's affectionate society.

In reflecting upon God's work in creation and what they took
it to imply about the nature of God, Christian believers came
to see that God was not an absent-minded initiator of a set of

determined processes to the outcome of which God was indifferent. On the contrary, God is a present reality for the world about which God cares absolutely. The way that Christian theologians later learned to put this was to say that God had committed God's self to the well-being of God's creation, and that this is what is meant by calling it a creation, not a happenstance.

The Christian community of faith, later called the Church, came into being out of the conversation among some Jews and others in the first century CE with Jesus, whom they came to believe was the Messiah and whom they called the Christ. Their astonishing experience of his teaching, his life and society, caused them to consider his death as revelatory of the life that they could actually live in the world. It led them, moreover, in the light of this to think very hard about the God to whom Jesus pointed as the source of his authority in life and death, in word and action. The result was that they came to believe – from their Jewish point of view an almost unbelievable claim – that the wholeness of God had been present in Jesus.

This transformed the way in which they talked about themselves, their world and God, because it implied that God could genuinely be known and loved by humankind because they and the world were known and loved by God. Moses may have said that no man could look on God and live; they came to hold the contrary opinion, that man in Christ had looked on God and lived. Indeed their faith amounted to the claim that it was only by recognizing that one could look on God that one could live! And what a life they claimed to envisage: an open life that welcomed all others, celebrated the real presence of God with his people and the whole world, a personal life of divinely human freedom for all people of faith.

Jesus by his death reveals the love of God

One might say that it was by his death that Jesus revealed the love of God for all to see. I want to say that, by the same token, the fact of death reveals to every person the love of God. Some traditions of human reflection have struggled to hold these

themes together. One thinks of romanticism, that literary movement born out of a reaction to the apparent reductionism of the
Enlightenment. It flourished between, say, 1770 and 1850 in
Europe. In the face of an individualistic interiorization of life
and a loss of any sense of knowing how things were in themselves, writers, especially poets such as Wordsworth, Coleridge
and Goethe felt that the human experience of creativity and love
was so personal and so fragile that death and love were held in
sharp mutual tension, but were in principle immutably bound
together. But it was the lostness implicit in their response to
death that paradoxically inspired them, not the hopefulness of
love itself.

'The Rime of the Ancient Mariner' encapsulates the themes.
The mariner tells his tale to all who will listen as his experience
compelled him to do. A ship on which he served is caught in ice.
As the ice breaks they spot an albatross, which thrills the crew
and seems to guide them through the fog towards what they
believe will be safety. On an impulse, the mariner shoots the
albatross and the ship is cursed. The ship travels north and is
becalmed in appalling equatorial heat in a rotting sea; as retribu-
tion for his inexplicable behaviour, the mariner has the body of
the dead albatross hung around his neck. A 'dead' ship comes
into view on which Death and Life-in-Death are playing dice,
which presages the death of all the crew except the mariner himself, who is saved. Inspired by the beauty of the world in which
he paradoxically finds himself, the albatross falls from the neck
of the mariner.

One may interpret the meaning behind and within the poem
in the following way. The sailors lose their lives because their
self-understanding was bound up with the business of blaming
another for their troubles. The ancient mariner blames himself.
Because he knows he is lost, he is free to find his way and ultimately accept salvation. His penance is that he must travel the
world and share his experience by telling his story to all, as a
means of arousing in them a reverence for all God's creatures.
By the lost all may be led to salvation: through death all may
find life. As Coleridge himself once said, 'The Poet is the man

made to solve the riddle of the universe.' The poet is drawn to the inside of things and grasps after what he sees with the intention of expressing its form in language. When once he has glimpsed the vision, he can no more keep it to himself than the cuckoo can keep silent. How can Christians give expression to the interiority of their faith so that others may share something of the life which will give them hope and joy?

Death puts life into perspective

From whatever point of view one regards death, its reality is undeniable; it defines life, affirms our personhood and puts things into perspective. But for death, we would have no opportunity of seeing life whole, and on that our capacity to be responsible and die a good death depends. Some further words of Heidegger are helpful.

> We may formulate in three theses the discussion of death up to this point: 1. There belongs to Dasein (*being there*) as long as it is, a 'not yet' which it will be – that which is constantly still outstanding; 2. The coming-to-its-end of what-is-not-yet-at-an-end (in which what is still outstanding is liquidated as regards its Being) has the character of no-longer-Dasein; 3. Coming-to-an-end implies a mode of Being in which the particular Dasein simply cannot be represented by somebody else.[71]

Three important points arise from Heidegger's words. First, the wholeness of life which death offers us must be accepted. Not to do so will take our life away from us and frustrate the focus on preparation for death. Second, let's remind ourselves what we mean by preparation, for it is nothing to do with a refocusing of living on life *after* death. Far from it: to prepare for a good death implies first and foremost living a good life now, for it is how we have lived our lives that will characterize our death. Life now is what we are released to enjoy when once we have come to terms with the fact that death *is,* must be accepted and is in principle liberating. Third, we are free to be ourselves; there is nobody left to blame, nobody to carry the can for us. Freedom came to the Ancient Mariner when that dawned on him.

When contemplating his father's death, Dylan Thomas urged him not to 'go gentle into that dark night', but to 'rage, rage against the dying of the light'.[72] I've a lot of sympathy with that perspective since it seems so natural to me – there will be a lot left undone, promises not fulfilled, thankfulness and gratitude unexpressed, books not read, friendships not celebrated, enemies not reconciled, gifts left unmade and words left unsaid. Quite enough to make one mad with guilt, regret and frustration! But that is not the point; as I have said above, 'There is always time' – a never-to-be forgotten thought! Let me suggest a way in which we can think about it.

The present

I alluded above to the Husserlian notion of 'extended present'. Husserl suggested that the actual moment of time had no literal reality because, to be intelligible at all, it must be assumed to include much that is past, and much that is to come. Since the 'present' occupies, as it were, no space, it is not subject to process and is therefore beyond conceptualization, let alone beyond influence even by affectionate courtesy. However, if we follow Husserl and think of the present as extended to include both the past and the future, then we can conceive of the dynamic energy locked into the black hole of the present, as potential as unbounded and creative. Thereby we recognize the present to be redeemable: indeed, only the present is redeemable. Now that is an encouraging thought! Nicholas Humphrey helps further when he discusses the notion of consciousness:

> Consciousness has a paradoxical dimension of temporal 'depth'. The present moment, the 'now' of sensations, is experienced as 'temporally thick'.
> . . .
> Suppose indeed that human beings travel through life as in a

'time ship,' that like a spaceship has a prow and a stern and *room inside* for us to move around.

Well, in that case we would not be talking about the 'present' as a physicist defines it. We might, however, be talking about the 'subjective present' as we actually experience it. The 'physical present,' strictly speaking, is a mathematical abstraction of infinitely short duration, and nothing happens in it. By contrast the 'subjective present' is arguably the carrier and *container* of our conscious life, and everything that ever happens to us happens *in it*.[73]

What I have in mind is that we should think of death as the God-given opportunity to gather up the whole of our personal life into the 'thick subjective present' so as to offer it to God with grateful affection. Actually, of course, the offering of ourselves that we make in death is voiceless; our voice will be lost 'in wonder, love and praise'. This thought merits closer attention.

The natural community of God and world: Creation and the Triune God

The Christian faith, as I understand it, affirms the natural community of God and the world: this is what we mean, in fact, when we refer to the world as God's creation. It offers to humankind a divine encounter such that we may come to see our wholeness, and indeed the wholeness of the whole world, as dependent upon God. This was not new with Jesus – he did not, as it were, bring God with him into the world or by some superhuman effort persuade God to come back to a world that God had abandoned. Jesus by his life and death showed us God and God's world as it really is; the world is of a kind where God could be known and loved. God has never been absent in such a manner as to require him at a later time to make up his mind whether to return to it or not. Such language makes no sense when used of God; time is not a category of experience that influences, let alone determines, how God behaves. God is here: indeed, to put it even more crisply, *God is*.

But what conception of God is it that we are talking about? Yes, God is committed to the redemptive creation of a world in which God may be encountered by humankind. But since we have talked above of God's aseity – God's dependence upon God's self for God's nature and being – how can we better characterize an approach to what it is for God to be God? In order to tackle this difficult, perhaps in reality impossible, question, Christian theologians have developed the doctrine of the Trinity. But how does that help us? Many have found it a doctrine that is easily ridiculed. One can imagine the conversation.

'Three Persons in One God, you say?'

'Yes, it is how we Christians talk of God's indivisibility in unity.'

'Really? Come again. That's how you talk of God's unity? But surely you are talking now of Three Persons, not one; how does such an idea possibly help to understand the unity of God?'

'Well, you see, it is a mystery, but one which illuminates the essential truth about God that Christians proclaim.'

'I don't see it. It seems to me that you are either asserting a contradiction – God is three persons and God is one person – or you are simply claiming that the term 'mystery' in some way allows you to claim that meaningless statements have a meaning really. Either way, you are not offering anything that a sensible person would find it worthwhile wrestling with.'

And so one might go on for ever. There are, of course, those who think it a simple and obvious matter. I remember an occasion when on holiday with my family in Cornwall we went to the local church on the Sunday. The preacher began his sermon by referring to the fact that it was Trinity Sunday. I thought this sounded promising since the subject was rarely tackled in my experience. However, my interest waned quickly when he continued, 'The Trinity has never caused me any difficulty and I don't suppose it has you, so we shall spend our time thinking about the suffering of the Third World and how we could do something about it.' I should have taken his telephone number, since any help in understanding the doctrine of the Trinity is always welcome.

But I think we have something to work on if we take seriously the thought of the eternal present as being 'thick time'. Perhaps we could say of God that since God is eternally present, God wraps up in God's self all that precedes any moment of time and everything that is potentially of the future. This would be a way of approaching what we meant when we referred to God as absolutely personal in his nature. Out of God's self there would be created all that could be and all that was, but each, both past and present, would be capable of transformation through participation in the lived-through experience of creation. The creation being all that God was making in creation and which was Other than God but which owed its existence to God's being. The God to whom we are referring is therefore a God who is free to give God's self to the world because God is 'at peace with God's self', content with the direction in which God is going, and confident that the nature of the creative spirit through which God engages with the creation is indeed redemptive. We talk through with one another this perspective on God in the light of our conviction that the world is focused upon the possibility of facilitating our becoming whole persons through encounter with God as God is in God's self: in particular, in response to our hearing the Word of God spoken in Christ and celebrated in the Church, the community of faith.

The speechless openness of death

In response to this vision of God in relation to the world, we gather up in death all that we are, and in that moment of truth make the offering of our personal selves. Death indeed can be said to define who and what we are, what we have stood for and what we have wanted. But death is more than the literal non-speaking of the human person; it is the (at last!) speechless openness of the human person in response to the loving voice of

God hitherto only dimly heard above and within the roar of the traffic of ordinary human affairs. What we have affirmed when we were baptized in the name of the Father and of the Son and of the Holy Spirit, what we have recalled and enjoyed in the eternal regularity of eucharistic celebration, 'This is my Body', that is indeed what in death we know once and for all to be truly 'the Real Presence'. What we have hoped for is true: *God is*. The ordinariness of our experience presents to us the divinely human dimensions of our humanity.

The life-giving Word of God that we are promised in death is that of the same God whose creation this is, who spoke in Jesus Christ, and who inspires every desire that stirs the human spirit to grasp after truth, justice, peace, understanding and wisdom. Everything coheres in that divinely human conversation which we have open to us through God's grace. We might put it thus. The vigorous, attractive speech of the Trinity engagingly extends itself and overflows in the Word of creation and the gradually extending work of the conversation of the Spirit to include all creaturely affairs: it assumes them into the stimulating interior conversation of the Trinity. In death, we gather up in our voiceless speech all that we are, and collapse, as it were, into the pent-up energy of a black hole, only to be released as we find ourselves included as a believing soul in the conversation of the Trinity. The speech of the Trinity is unsayable in our day-to-day language, but is gradually recognizable and appreciated through a process of iterative action leading to the formation of habits of believing and doing. To this must be added the freedom of interpretation that gives to each individual the opportunity to contribute personally to the richness of God's creative purpose, a contribution that will be written in truthful speaking and virtuous action, in picture and imagination.

Behold, I am with you always

The mutuality of this process is reflected in the language of Christian spirituality. Jesus, the Word of God, promises to be with us and to dwell in us always. God, the Father, calls us to God's self and invites us to be one in God's self. Paul develops the image of a Christian as being 'in Christ', and of the Church as the Body of Christ with the members as God's limbs. It is not that we contribute to the Being of God or that God is in some way defective, lacking a dimension that we can add. Rather, it is that there are aspects of God's incarnate self that depend upon our speech if the conversation of the Trinity is to have full voice in the world of the human chorus. Hence, in order to continue and develop God's conversation with the world, we have been given our affections, our will and our intelligence to pursue truth in all relevant matters.

Above all, there is the matter of prayer, for prayer and meditation can be said to be ways in which in intention and faith we approach formally the matter of conversation with God. It is in prayer that we try to be quiet, to listen, to be at peace. Not easy. There will be intellectual issues. How can there be a risen Christ? What on earth – I use the expression advisedly – can that mean? And perhaps we recall conversations, stories that help. Moral issues. Surely it is right to pursue stem-cell research, given the promise that it offers to sufferers of diseases that are at present incurable? Is the good always the best? Matters of injustice. We are stirred by the apparent injustice of the treatment of homosexuals, but what can I do about it? Human greed seems to be denying to so many the very necessities of life, but what can I do? How can I find the words to say what I mean and be understood? All these things and many more: personal concerns, anxiety about our family, fear of international conflict, loss of job, old age, illness, and many more. And, let us not forget, all those wonderful things that we recall with infinite pleasure: all the happinesses, gifts, joys and treasures that we have enjoyed. All these matters are gathered up into prayer because at the heart of prayer is a profound silence when we place into God's hands all that we have in the hope that God can do something with it. We hope that it contributes in some way to God's redemptive creativity, that it can be heard to be a way in which we are taking part in and extending God's conversation with the world. One might say that prayer is a pale attempt to anticipate that presence with our Father through the Son in the power of the Holy Spirit that we are promised in the Beatific Vision. To the extent that we do – and it may be rare – it will be a 'mountaintop experience', something which common sense will bring us down from back into reality. But notwithstanding any disappointment we may experience, it will be a reality that we are perhaps a little more encouraged to see as *also* the place where God is.

Angelo Roncalli, Pope John XXIII, remembered seeing on the wall of the presbytery of his parish priest when he was a boy, words which he never forgot. They are said to be words of St Bernard. They have something to teach us:

> Hear all; believe a few; honour all.
> Do not believe everything you hear;
> Do not do everything you can;
> Do not give everything you have;
> Do not say everything you know.[74]

These words could well be written on our hearts as we attempt to transform our own lives after the pattern of Christ so that we have something to offer in him. Of course, part of our praying should itself be focused upon our hope to 'die well'. This dimension of prayer was more common in times past. Take the following as an example:

> Holy angels of Heaven, I beg you to assist me who am about to pass out of this world, to strongly preserve and keep me from all my enemies, and receive my soul into your blessed company: and particularly you, the good blessed angel which has been my continual guardian, appointed by God.[75]

Perhaps these are not words that carry the right ring in our twenty-first-century environment. I'm not sure: I rather like them myself, although, as I've said above, I don't really understand the world of angels, let alone a 'guardian angel'. But I do understand the freshness of the hope that we are not alone in death, that we are included within a pattern of redemptive creativity that is God's work; and if it helps to put that in terms of being accompanied by a 'guardian angel' appointed by God, that does justice to my feelings about human life, and I'm all for it.

In any case, it is a good discipline to try to write a prayer that you would want to pray yourself in contemplation and anticipation of the presence of death. Many hymns have that thought at their heart and may be sung with the angels with heartfelt thanks and joyful anticipation. Here's one of Isaac Watts's great hymns which makes the point:

> I'll praise my Maker while I've breath;
> And when my voice is lost in death,
>   Praise shall employ my nobler powers:
> My days of praise shall ne'er be past,
> While life and thought and being last,
>   Or immortality endures.

> Happy are they whose hopes rely
> On Israel's God! He made the sky,
>   And earth and sea, with all their train:
> His truth for ever stands secure;
> He saves the oppressed, he feeds the poor,
>   And none shall find his promise vain.

> The Lord pours eyesight on the blind;
> The Lord supports the fainting mind;
>   He sends the labouring conscience peace;
> He helps the stranger in distress,
> The widow and the fatherless,
>   And grants the prisoner sweet release.

> I'll praise my Maker while I've breath;
> And when my voice is lost in death,
>   Praise shall employ my nobler powers;
> My days of praise shall ne'er be past,
> While life and thought and being last,
>   Or immortality endures.

(Isaac Watts, 1674–1748, based on Psalm 146)

If we believed that, the world would be a different place, would it not? But that's the point! The truth is that the world is like that; it is just that we find it so hard to accept that it is and therefore to base our lives on living it out. Thank God that in death we shall know, even as we are known.

5

Personal Identity and the Soul

The soul in question

So who or what are we? What is this me that will be 'saved'?
Who is the 'you' that will inherit eternal life? I cannot remember
the last time I had a conversation about the soul, or indeed a time
when anybody asked me about it. It is as if political correctness
now requires us not to mention the topic for fear of being accused
of being out-of-date, or just plain ignorant. When did you last
hear a sermon on the subject? Yet the term is familiar from the
Authorised Version of the Bible, has played a part in Christian
theological reflection about what it is to be a person, and continues to be a part of Christian worship in hymns and prayers. Take,
for example, this familiar hymn based on Psalm 103 that finds a
place in many hymnbooks and is still regularly sung:

> Praise, my soul, the King of heaven;
>   To his feet thy tribute bring.
> Ransomed, healed, restored, forgiven,
>   Who like thee his praise should sing?
>   Praise him! Praise him!
> Praise the everlasting King![76]

(Henry Francis Lyte, 1793–1847)

Have you really no idea what you are talking about when you
sing the words, 'Praise, *my soul*, the King of heaven'? I don't
think so, though I hope you think about it and weigh up carefully
what you do mean. But nevertheless, the question hangs over us
– what do we mean by the word 'soul'? It is not transparent.

73

Look at Isaac Watts' great hymn usually sung at Easter but appropriate for any occasion of Christian worship. It is biblically based on the New Testament, Galatians 6.14:

> When I survey the wondrous cross,
>   On which the Prince of Glory died,
> My richest gain I count but loss,
>   And pour contempt on all my pride.
>
> Forbid it, Lord, that I should boast
>   Save in the death of Christ my God;
> All the vain things that charm me most,
>   I sacrifice them to his blood.
>
> See from his head, his hands, his feet,
>   Sorrow and blood flow mingled down;
> Did e'er such love and sorrow meet,
>   Or thorns compose so rich a crown?
>
> His dying crimson, like a robe,
>   Spreads o'er his body on the tree;
> Then am I dead to all the globe,
>   And all the globe is dead to me.
>
> Were the whole realm of nature mine,
>   That were a present far too small;
> Love so amazing, so divine,
>   Demands my soul, my life, my all.[77]

(Isaac Watts, 1674–1748)

I don't believe that we sing this as prayerfully as we do without having some understanding of the word 'soul' as Watts uses it here. It is in apposition to 'my life', and 'my all', and, as it were, allows me to sum up in one simple word all that I am – my life and my all, everything that I am. Quite apart from the familiarity of the word in hymns, there are over 700 times when the word is used in the Authorised Version of the Old Testament, and some 50 or so in the New Testament.

But notwithstanding my claim that the word has meaning for those who know how to use it, many dismiss the concept as meaningless, valueless or of merely historical interest. Daniel Dennett says, 'I think the idea of a soul is a curious fossil trace of the desire to treat ourselves as absolute.'[78] Clearly, too, that swashbuckling hero of popular irrational anti-intellectualism, Richard Dawkins, has no time to waste on considering whether the term 'soul' might have a significant meaning for human self-understanding. He ridicules, for example, William of Wykeham's motives when he endowed his own College (New College, Oxford), in 1379 because although they may have included a commitment to educational aspiration, they were primarily directed towards making provision for the salvation of his own soul. To this end William of Wykeham left money for ten chaplains, three clerks and 16 choristers whose purpose was to pray for his soul; indeed, were the College's other income to fail, his will determined that they were to be retained. His immortal soul was to be saved at the cost of any educational purpose. The silliness must now be apparent to all and, as Dawkins sees it, the comparison between the purpose of a flourishing education institution and the saving of a single soul grotesque.[79]

However, perhaps we should not be too dismissive of their rejection of the idea of a soul and questioning of its meaning: it could even help us to refocus our thinking about what it means to think about who or what we are. What I take to be the misunderstandings that lie behind their comments are all too common. In one sense, the term 'soul' is a surviving fossil from another age; in another, Richard Dawkins is right to regard as silly the way in which William of Wykeham's will provides for the eternal life of his soul. For what many see as implied by the term 'soul' is more consistent with Greek philosophical thought than with the biblical tradition. Thus, for example, the soul is not something *apart* from the body – the Hebrew *nephesh* has no such meaning; the very idea was foreign to the Israelite mind. So the conventional view that the soul is some *thing* that in some mysterious way or another inhabits the physical body and at the moment of death somehow escapes from the body is not what the Christian means when referring to the soul.

Indeed, when it has been thought of in this way it has led to very strange theories and what to Christians are very odd and misleading questions. Thus, for example, since in dissection of the human body we have come across no evidence to support the view that there is substance or matter that we could identify as the soul, the soul must be immaterial. The assumption that the soul is a purely spiritual entity may have satisfied some, but it created one enormous, insoluble problem. How could a spiritual entity, even if in some sense it existed, act upon the material body as is claimed?

Descartes, who may with equal plausibility be considered the last of the medieval philosophers and/or the first of the moderns, took up this question. The way in which he approached it, while of its time, nevertheless has some elements that are helpful. When distinguishing between the perceptions which we attribute to the body and those which we refer to the soul, Descartes talks of those which we associate with the limbs such as pain or hunger and those which cannot be identified with any particular part of the body but rather with the whole of the self. He puts it this way:

> But in order to understand all these things more perfectly, we need to recognise that the soul is really joined to the whole body, and that we cannot properly say that it exists in any one part of the body to the exclusion of the others. For the body is a unity which is in a sense indivisible because of the arrangement of its organs, these being so related to one another that the removal of any one of them renders the whole body defective. And the soul is of such a nature that it has no relation to extension, or to the dimensions of other properties of the matter of which the body is composed: it is related solely to the whole assemblage of the body's organs. This is obvious from our inability to conceive of a half or a third of a soul, or of the extension which a soul occupies. Nor does the soul become any smaller if we cut off some part of the body, but

it becomes completely separate from the body when we break up the assemblage of the body's organs.[80]

Descartes' understanding of the soul as related to the body as a whole is very helpful and, as we shall see, closely related to a biblical understanding. Moreover, it is one that we can work with today as we try to come to terms again with a notion of 'the whole person'. I do not believe that I am the sum of my various physical interactions with the public world of human experience; I have a sense of personal identity which is over and above this, which I bring to bear on my experience and by means of which I hold it together and begin to make sense of it. Descartes took seriously the essential interaction of the soul with the whole of what was expressed in the human physical body and believed that there must be some physical organ which itself interacted with every other dimension of the body's behaviour: he identified this with the pineal gland.

However illuminating, Descartes' association of the soul with the sense a person has of his whole self has been unhelpful, in fact, since it is based in principle upon an assumed dualism of mind and body, it is a bifurcation that the Christian tradition is unable to defend; on the contrary, it affirms the wholeness of human being *and* its dependence upon the community of both God and the world of God's creation if it is to flourish. The body and the soul are not two independent natures that are mysteriously brought to impact upon one another; they are in fact a unity, two ways of expressing the single nature of what it is to be human. One might best express this unity by saying that human being is *body* in relation to the physical world seen as independent of God, but *soul* in respect of an appreciation that true human nature can only be understood as part of a divinely natural world which is related to God as its Redemptive Creator.

In the image of God

Human personhood is relational and dynamic in its nature; it takes its character from being formed by God in God's image. Human being is therefore full of hope since it is born free to share with God in building with God a world of joy, peace and faith. To this end, humankind has the essential curiosity to want to understand the world, so as to contribute to its creation, to share the divine concern for its well-being and desire to build a partnership with God and creation. This dynamic vision of what it is to be human is often contrasted with Existentialism, a philosophy that flourished in a throwaway and confused post-war society. But for many an existentialist perspective seems to imply a fixed and static view of human nature. Certainly existentialism can be taken this way, and in Christian theology often has been, but if we were to say that the essential nature of what it is to be human shaped in the image of God *is* that it is dynamic and relational, we should do it more justice. Surely it must be clear that to be made in the image of God simply means that humankind shares the dynamic creativity of the divine nature and the desire to express it in sympathetic concern for the 'other's well-being'. Above all, there is no fixed end, no utopia, no 'final solution' to which we are directed by God and to which we are called to take others, by force if necessary; only loving progress towards a fullness of relationship with ourselves, one another, the world and God. Utopias are all anathema to the Christian tradition – or should be![81]

Whatever else God might be, God is not static or fixed. He is Personal Being. This may be thought to be in conflict with the view that God is changeless. There is not space here to discuss this. Suffice it to say for our purpose now, the changelessness of God is affirmed in God's nature as the One who is committed always to the well-being of the other, whatever that demands in personal suffering and pain.[82]

Responsible human living

Looked at in this way, how should we develop and interpret our responsibilities as human souls? We act under the authority of God who has created and continues to create the world of which we are a part and in whose creation we share. A simple interpretation assumes that it means we should do as God tells us. But such a naïve interpretation of 'obedience' is thoroughly misleading: it has grown out of a gross misunderstanding of the story of the Fall. The obedience to which we are called requires understanding which comes only from hard work; it is active, not passive. Above all, it assumes an understanding of ourselves as based in the relational environment in which we find ourselves, our divine–human world.

Certainly to try to live one's life as if God had nothing to do with the world or us will lead to an introverted and fearful attitude to our own lives. Adam, in the story of the Garden of Eden, is described as succumbing to the illusion that he can do what he wants without regard to the fact that there are consequences for others including himself and Eve if he acts as if God does not exist. It is not so, as he finds out rather smartly: there are consequences. He is immediately excluded from the completeness of the divinely natural world, and all creation with him. To live a genuinely human life requires respect for the divinely natural world of which we are a part. To live as if it was all 'divine' or as if it was all 'secular', let alone as if everything is mine, is to live without the light of true knowledge. Human beings can only live out their lives wholly when they accept responsibility for the world and for other members of the human race, in the light of the fact that all are members of God's divine–human world.

Such responsible obedience, of course, implies that responsibility has been delegated: for delegated responsibility to be exercised at all, not just well and properly, both the authority that gives responsibility and the agent to whom responsibility has been given will have to understand that they are free to act – within limits. It seems as if we should consider God, as Christians believe him to be, as the original, best and only true manager. God retains some responsibility for God's self, God must be true to God's own nature – in the last resort he 'carries the can'. But he delegates *really* and does not interfere or second-guess what choices human beings may choose to make.

There are nevertheless limits to our delegated authority. Some are clear. We cannot act in contravention of the 'laws of nature', though there is important debate about what these 'laws' are and how they are to be interpreted. Certainly, however, we cannot be in two places at once, we cannot fly, we are not immortal nor can we achieve immortality. On the other hand, our freedoms are huge. We can understand the world and apply our knowledge. We can harness some natural processes and discover through experience what is profitable for our own and the world's well-being. We can learn to understand and sympathize with another's well-being. We can fall in love and make with others a success of our lives. Indeed, almost all successful enterprise is a joint activity.

There is controversy, of course, about what we should do, and much conversation is necessary to resolve disputes. For myself, however, I cannot see that there can be limits to scientific research, notwithstanding the fact that experience shows us that we shall find it very difficult if not impossible to resist setting about the risky business of applying what we know. Hence, for example, I am personally in favour of stem-cell research, incineration of organic waste material to produce energy, animal experimentation if it is for human benefit, and nuclear power; but I understand why there is public debate about them and why there will need to be strict systems of regulation. Of course, the outcomes will be unclear; there are uncertainties involved. But then, I believe that human being is empowered to be responsibly venturesome.

In exercising genuine judgement about controversial matters, we have to attend not only to our own personal interests, but to those of other people, the physical environment and the total environment of human concern which includes God: naturally I am unlikely (nor is any other individual) to have the whole picture at my fingertips, nor to be capable of predicting all the outcomes! But the fact is that we are free to learn, to experiment, to make judgements in the light of our understanding and to develop policies to implement them. These are all necessary if we are to grow in knowledge of ourselves, of our world and of God.

Accountability

We shall quite properly be held to account for our choices by one another, by the world, and by God: hence the importance of revisiting decisions in the light of experience and applying also to them our growing understanding of what it is to live under the authority of God. There is a role therefore in our Christian life together for the scientist, both physical and social, the technologist, the businessperson, the politician, the economist, the theologian, the artist and many other areas of professional enquiry. The scientist will uncover 'the facts' as far as is possible and test them: the technologist will propose ways in which to apply the knowledge acquired; the businessperson will attempt to exploit them, and the economist will strive to make the potential benefits available to as many people as possible. The politician will try to develop institutions which provide for public accountability in political systems and legal frameworks. The theologian works at the public understanding of God and God's relationship with the world in the light of the knowledge and experience we are gaining from living in it. The artist offers the liberation of the world of the imagination so that we are not bogged down in any conventional pattern of thinking in any area of enquiry, nor confined by the past in deciding what to do in the future. It is a fantastically exciting thing to be a human being! It is something which we all too frequently forget as we allow stress to eat at our curiosity, and safety-first attitudes to limit our sense of the freedom which we in fact enjoy.

The theologian has at hand useful terminology with which to grasp this responsibility and make it real. At the heart of it all lies the experience of trust. To see this in perspective we have first to recognize that God, having in creation delegated responsibility to us, trusts us. Hence, though we are capable of mistakes, we are allowed to make them on the presumption that we will learn from our experience. But through it all we are assured of God's loving-kindness, his ever-present love, and the courtesy of his absolute attention. Punishment, let alone retributive justice, does not lie at the heart of the world's experience of God as enjoyed by humankind. Not even a sparrow falls without God's attention! God is redemptively creative; God is always working to bring God's self to our attention, to remind us of God's presence, so that we are not depressed, frustrated or irritated by the unwelcome consequences of our own misunderstandings and mistaken choices.

We can talk about this, and often do, as forgiveness. We think of it most usually in personal terms, and quite rightly: it is the whole *me* who seeks forgiveness for error; it is I who am forgiven, not my foot or my brain. But of course it is also 'personal' when, as we should, we think of forgiveness as we find it in the renewability of nature and the new opportunities that it gives to us to make all things new. It may be very hard to take things this way if you are trying to eradicate Japanese knotweed from several hectares of land, as the engineers are doing on the site designated for the stadium for the 2012 London Olympics: but it is so.[83] One's attitude to the 'natural world' is transformed when one conceives of it in appropriate personal terms.

God's trust in humankind

There are many dimensions to God's trust of us, but the central point is that trust is the absolute opposite of fear. We can afford to be bold in our decision-making; we can trust our experience and build up our wisdom; we can acquire good habits of thought and action. Fear will inhibit, undermine confidence and eventually destroy us because it renders us unable to trust, which is a denial of our true nature, which is trusting and trustful. There are, unfortunately, countless examples in our society where young people grow up out of relationship with themselves. Their trust having been betrayed by parents, friends and peer groups, they have to rely on selves that they may not know, and a view of the world that threatens their ability to know themselves as trusting, trustful and affectionate persons. But it is possible for them to know the forgiving nature of the world, public and private, human and divine, because it is personal and the creation of God.

There arises from this view of the divine–human nature of the world open to our enjoyment an expectation that we will trust one another and build patterns of dynamic relationship based upon delegation. This is how God's own humankind made in God's image shares God's redemptive creativity. This we are not very good at – with enormous destructive consequences. We see it in the building up of suspicion between the generations, parents and children, between nations, between the genders, the races and the religions, even between those professional persons who are informed by and are expert in different disciplines. Instead of seeing that all are one in the sense that there is one world, one human race and one God, and that therefore what we are seeking to do in our lives is to live out the consequences of our oneness, we resort to destructive use of power in order to secure what we believe to be our own interests at the expense of others. Adam all over again! Hardly the way to go, if we are to realize our own true natures and be true to ourselves! Holding things together may be superficially harder than trying to live our lives according to a particular set of opinions which we accept as true without question, but since we shall be more true to ourselves if we try to do so, it will bring us greater satisfaction in the end – because it will be based upon the truth that all things do hang together.

The apostle Paul thought very hard about the impact that his faith in the risen Christ and his revelation of God had made upon him, as even slight acquaintance with his epistles makes clear. He had struggled when he lived under the Law. As it now seemed to him, he had then been trying to be obedient to an impossible demand if he was to live in the light of his understanding of the loving kindness of Yahweh. Yahweh had certainly redeemed his chosen people but their deliberate eschewing of his ways had led to their (temporary) punishment and frequent despair as they waited for Yahweh's return as the Messiah to rescue them. There were fathers, heroes, prophets and kings whose examples inspired hope in their tradition; there was expectation and often even genuine faith and hope. But that was all in straight contrast with what he now felt: when he 'saw' Jesus, he believed he had found the fulfilment of the Law and the Prophets; he was transported to a different environment – morally, intellectually, spiritually and above all theologically.

It was as if he had read John Robinson's article in the *Observer* newspaper before the publication of *Honest to God* and accepted that 'our image of God must go'.[84] God was not 'away from home' until the people learned to behave themselves; he was not unwilling to answer letters; God was not incommunicado. God was not unknowable, though God may not be completely known. Neither the Jewish people, nor the world of which they were the chosen representatives, was cut off from God and required, in the interim, to satisfy performance criteria if God was to make his way back. There were no criteria of that kind, indeed in no way could humankind 'satisfy' the requirements of God if that was how living and loving God were to be thought of. There was no room for such moral and intellectual reductionism in God's world.

Actually, as St Paul now saw it, it was all the other way round; he had got it all back to front. God had never withdrawn from the world; far from God being absent, God was already present in the world with humankind. They had not known how to recognize God and lacked the language to express clearly what their experience added up to. To put it this way is not somehow to reduce it to a simple matter; having the right language at one's disposal is crucial to every area of enquiry. Indeed, that is what dawned on St Paul when he found that he could not take his eyes off Jesus; he was drawn in to give his whole attention to Jesus' teaching, death and resurrection. How could he say what he saw? How could he make a reality of it in his life? Paul intuited that there was nothing left – there never had been – for humanity to achieve on its own. It was all done, '*Tetelestai* – It is finished'.[85] And it was! As the story of creation had it, 'God saw everything that he had made, and indeed, it was very good.'[86] Very good, indeed!

Paul saw, perhaps for the first time, what was implied in this story culminating in the claim that the whole world of God's creation was very good; God was at home with God's people in God's world; they were in partnership with one another. This apparently unbelievable association of God and the world of humankind had been thought an out-of-this-world claim to make in Judaism; so much so that it was thought by many to amount to nothing less than blasphemy. Yet that was to misunderstand it all. As Walter Brueggemann has shown, in fact the whole of the Jewish tradition as it developed in the Old Testament was all about partnership: partnership between Israel and Yahweh, the human person and Yahweh, the nations and Yahweh, creation and Yahweh.[87] No wonder that Paul, as far as we can see, did not think of this dynamic vision as superseding or bypassing Judaism, any more than Jesus had himself; rather, Paul saw his 'new' faith as fulfilling, completing, renewing and developing Jewish hopes. This 'new' faith was the realization of Jewish hopes. Hence also, of course, if we are to get inside the meaning of Christian faith and inhabit the world it conjures up, it is still important not to put aside Judaism but to hold together both the Old and the New Testaments. At the same time I do not wish, any more than I think Paul did, to confuse Judaism with Christianity; they are two independent living traditions that nevertheless at the same time should live in a symbiotic, mutually nourishing and supportive relationship.

Living in God's divine–human world

This is the perspective in which we should explore the relationship of body and spirit, body and soul. To cut us off from awareness of the totality of the divine–human world of which we are a part, and to live apart from it, is to try to flourish as a body. To attempt to do so, as St Paul points out, is death, literally and physically so. 'Here we have no continuing city', words which T. S. Eliot put in the mouth of the Chorus in *Murder in the Cathedral* – and we know it. No Christian, any more than any other human being, can sensibly deny it; it is a fact. However, human life is not defined simply in terms of the body; there is the larger dimension of the divine in which the world of the body is set, and the language of theology in which that is grasped and best expressed. Given such a dimension, we can see ourselves not merely as body, but as soul; that is, as a self in relation to God. Insofar as I *am* a soul (not insofar as I *have* a soul – to speak in such a way is to make a crucial mistake, what Gilbert Ryle called a 'category mistake'), I conceive of myself as *being* in (not 'having') a relationship with God. That is what I am encouraged to nourish in my life by trying to work out what it means to love God, to live out that relationship in my life with others, to treat them and the world with dignity, by making room in myself for that which is other than myself and allowing myself to be welcomed by others, therefore sharing their experiences and empathizing with them.

To talk of being with and feeling with others is far different and more energizing, more real, than simply trying to help them or offering assistance, though it implies that we will certainly do that if we can. It means also accepting the pain which is involved in being in the image of God and delegating to them their lives with all the suffering that may be entailed for me, so that they can enjoy the new relationship promised them in their creating – by me and by God. It can be an awful thing to have to recognize it, but the fact is that one cannot help those who do not want to be helped, any more than one can teach somebody who does not wish to learn.

A natural grounding for the experience of self and the soul

I have talked so far of a divine–human world, and of the human person as being 'body' and therefore subject to death in relation to the physical world conceived of as apart from God, and as 'soul' in respect of association with God and the opportunity to share in the divine life. It raises the important question whether there are helpful ways of putting our understanding of 'soul' into the process of emergent human life in the world. I believe there are.

So, where should we begin? Current discussion of consciousness and self-consciousness has potentially an important bearing on the understanding of our individuality and the Christian notion of the soul. Susan Blackmore, in a recently published series of interviews with scholars, asks several of her interlocutors whether the study of human consciousness and self-consciousness had changed them or their view of human life.[88] The question provoked a range of responses. The fact that several agree that it has impacted upon their views of themselves is intriguing since that is exactly what I am claiming for the understanding of the person and the soul in Christian theology. The divine–human world that we claim is humankind's natural environment and the personal engagement with learning that is involved transforms one's understanding of oneself and the life that is open to one. To 'see' that the world in which one has life is of divine origin is to open up new opportunities, new dimensions and fresh hopes; it stimulates us to speak a whole new language. Dom. Sebastian Moore wrote a book about it, *God Is a New Language*, but he has gone further in his thinking since then. He now talks of the new language giving the individual who learns to speak it a new consciousness.[89] Hence, of course, to teach theology is very demanding, for one is educating a person, not simply passing on information. Actually, when one thinks about it, this is or should be a feature of all genuine education.

Perhaps in the light of this reflection we should think of one's soul as an offering to God of all that one is conscious of being – a person who *is* in partnership with God. But what does this amount to? Does this take us any further? Have we made any progress? For if the term 'soul' is hardly a regular matter of public discussion, to talk of consciousness is itself problematic, and self-consciousness even more so. Recent discussion of the topic is extremely interesting. Among all the controversy in the field, I find the work of Nicholas Humphrey the most intriguing and suggestive when he addresses the question of consciousness and its purpose.[90]

Humphrey begins with the matter of human perception and argues that it is a purely physical process in which sensation plays no part. There is illuminating experimental data to support this view. There are, he argues, two aspects to the experience of perception. There is, first, the *objective* phenomenon of a patch of colour – there it is, a patch of colour that is red. And there is, second, the *subjective* fact that I am seeing a patch of colour, and it is red. But there is even more to it than that, because there is also the additional fact that I am conscious that I can see red.

The interesting feature is that the sensation of consciousness of a colour patch and the objective fact that the subject perceives a colour patch out there are two quite independent phenomena. The significance of this becomes apparent when one considers the implications of experiments that Humphrey carried out on a monkey called Helen. When her primary visual cortex at the back of the brain had been removed, she seemed to be completely blind. However, notwithstanding this deprivation, she appeared to be able to see, because in playing with her Humphrey noticed she was clearly watching what was going on. In the absence of the possibility of conversation no further progress could be made; monkeys cannot report their subjective experience. However, Weiskrantz, Humphrey's doctoral supervisor in Cambridge, continued experiments with persons who had suffered damage to their visual cortex and who were to all intents and purposes blind. They too showed evidence that they could 'see' in the sense that they adjusted their behaviour in relation to their visual field. Most interesting, however, was what they had to say about it. While they had no sensation of being able to see, they could still guess the position and shape of objects. The phenomenon, now known as blindsight, has been confirmed in sufficient cases for the evidence to be accepted. The implication is, therefore, that visual perception is independent of and antecedes the sensation of seeing. If this is really so, and the evidence that it is so continues to grow, then what purpose does sensation play?

Humphrey puts it like this:

> Our question, . . . was this; if sensation is not involved directly in perception, what *is* it involved in? What is *the point* of it? From the analysis of blindsight, a raft of answers has become apparent. What sensation does is to track the subject's *personal interaction* with the external world – creating the sense each person has of being present and engaged, lending a hereness, a nowness, a me-ness to the experience of the present moment.[91]

But Humphrey speculates that there is more. He introduces to his discussion the idea of a 'thick present' that we have noted above from Husserl, that we borrow from the past and the future to create an extended present. He observes that Monet, for example, in his pursuit of his art, talked of the importance of hanging on to each moment a little longer so as to be able to make proper use of it. The suggestion is that a sense of self is gradually built up by these 'conscious' experiences to give the impression that there is more to being human than mere physical substance; a human being is to be clearly distinguished from the environment in which he or she exists; a human being is a person.

> Suppose that, at a relatively late stage of human evolution, after the thick moment of consciousness has already become firmly established as an anchor for the Self, variant genes arise whose effect is to give the conscious Self just the extra twist that leads the human mind to form an exaggeratedly grandiose view of its own nature. Suppose, in other words, that, while as Clark says 'the self and its experience' is and ever

will be 'just a bit of the world suitably organized', *this* bit of the world becomes reorganized precisely so as to impress the subject with its *out-of-this-world* qualities. Then suppose that these individuals who are so impressed, those who fall for the illusion, tend to have longer and more productive lives.[92]

The implication that Humphrey draws from this is that consciousness matters to us because it is its function to matter: it is a means whereby we have encouraged ourselves to struggle with vigour to survive – to be ourselves – in an evolutionary framework which has given us the idea that we have something to live for – the universe exists for our benefit.

This interpretation of the evidence at our disposal about the nature of consciousness is only one among many, and I am certainly not qualified to argue about it one way or the other. However, the fact that we can set an intriguing account of the emergence of consciousness, and particularly of self-consciousness, into an evolutionary framework is very interesting and encouraging. Humphrey's use of the terms 'over-exaggeratedly grandiose', 'illusion' and 'out-of-this-world' are no part of the actual theory except insofar as he believes that they have been useful for human evolutionary development. They are based upon the assumption that he brings to his account of his interesting work that the world of human experience is entirely explicable in 'scientific terms' and that therefore to make anything else of it is not only unhelpful, but also illusory and false. This judgement goes far beyond the evidence. Putnam and many others who take scientific enquiry with due seriousness would disagree, as we have seen above.

As a matter of fact I agree about the use of 'out-of-this-world'; it is very unhelpful and misleading. On the contrary, I want to set this theory within the framework of a world that is naturally and wholly divine–human. I regard the theory of evolution to be as near to an incontrovertible fact as we could possibly imagine the employment of the scientific method(s) capable of producing. To be able to set the emergence of human self-consciousness within a natural framework of explanation is what I would expect and hope for. How could it possibly be anything else? There is nothing which comes 'from outside', and nothing which is in this sense 'out-of-this-world'. However, we do more justice to the world in which we find ourselves and to humankind as we experience it, by taking ourselves with the seriousness that we have come to think we deserve. As Christians have come to see it, the natural world of creation involves the conception of it as divinely human. This imaginative interpretation of experience provides the intellectual, moral and aesthetic framework in which to set all human understanding of the world and of the self. Perhaps we are partners with God in his redemptive creativity, and, in the making of our souls, our sense of self. From this arises the fact that potentially people 'make' by their lives something of significance to offer to God when we gather up all that we are in the 'thick moment' of death. We may call it a soul for shorthand, provided we understand the term; we may call it ourselves. We may think of it as everything we are, in relationship with God. But, like memory or affection, it arises naturally in our world and makes us aware of the persons we are.

It is certainly of profound interest that we should have available to us a view which is not based upon the thought that the idea of a soul's survival of death emerged from a fear of death, but because it was, and is, useful to life, to living our lives. That's good, and exactly what I would expect as a Christian theologian, and hope for as a Christian believer.

Persons in relation

There is one other dimension implicit in what has been said but which needs to be made explicit. My existence is not a separate individual reality. I am not a private, discrete person who has somehow to find out how to make a relationship with other private individuals, in their discrete worlds. On the contrary, I am in relationship, actually in many relationships from the moment of my conception. It is one of the facts implicit in sexual reproduction. We are a product of what we are made from, itself a union of two persons themselves in relation with the world and other people from their very beginning. Far from it being the case that my life is an attempt to make relationships, it is an attempt first to appreciate the relations in which I find myself and into which I am born. My development as a person, as I begin to appreciate what or who I am, depends upon the willing delegation of authority by parents and others, my absorption of the relationships into which I am introduced by my education which – if it is to be as creative as it could be – will be lifelong, and my willingness to take advantage of the authority which is delegated to me to take imaginative risks. Too little delegation and I shall be cramped in my style, too much and I shall fall foul of my ambition and overstep the mark. In either case, I shall lose the ability and the willingness to be venturesome because the world in which I live will be limited by my experience: I shall make the transcendental deduction and presume that the world I think I know is the world as it really is.

In fact, the process whereby I can become myself depends upon my capacity to make room for that which is the other – another person, another understanding, another perspective. A self who can do that is also, of course, of evolutionary interest: it is how we might contribute to the development of humankind. That is a matter of love that, as we can see from the life of Christ (at least as far as the Christian sees it and understands him), is also instantiated in the ordinary world of the divine–human creation. He, I believe, is the major contribution to the evolution of the human race because he reveals – that is, points to, shows up, and images – the nature of the relationships that characterize genuine human life and the true character of the soul. That he did by confirming the human–divine nature of the one world which humankind inhabits. He did so by affirming the real presence of God. God in the personal nature of creating affirms the other than God, makes room in God's self for the other and confirms in Christ the freedom of the other to recognize its genuine nature. Humankind, made in the image of God, is able to realize God's presence, to affirm the 'Other' and to become aware of the human self in all its fullness as a physical, thinking, emotional, spiritual being.

Of course, when I ask myself whether this is true – and I often do – I find that I still have to base my answer on what I think about the nature of God as well as what I believe about the nature of humankind and the world in which the human race is set. Whether it makes sense to talk in the way I have chosen to do in this chapter depends upon taking seriously the considered reports of all scholarly enquiry about human experience, the capacity to enjoy the world for its beauty, and the pleasurable society of others including family and friends. My perspective on these matters is constantly changing and a matter of lifelong commitment to finding out. It also depends ultimately upon the answer to the question of God's existence. And that is what I am dying to find out!

6

Living in Communion

It is often said that the one occasion in life when one is essentially, inevitably and absolutely alone, is in death. I do not believe that this is the case: it is based upon a misunderstanding. One may, of course, be on one's own in a physical sense; one may literally die by oneself. As it happens, for example, one may die in one's sleep while away from home in a hotel, be by oneself in a hospital bed or be killed by a sniper's bullet in Baghdad. But that sort of 'aloneness', being by oneself, is not what the Christian means by being alone. For the Christian, being alone would have to carry with it something of the overtone of abandonment, put on one side, separated from all meaning and sense. As the Christian contemplates the circumstances of human life, such an event is impossible. One may experience events in one's life that seem to isolate one; one may try to put oneself into a category of one and pursue a life of individual gratification without regard for anything or anyone else. Even this will only succeed for a limited period of time; one is bound to fail. Our human life, in one sense or another *every* human life, is one of relationships. And the moment of truth in death is no exception.

The biblical tradition of life with God is one of relationship. From beginning to end it bears testimony to the life of humankind being lived in interdependent relationship with God and the whole of creation. This manifests itself in the necessity to get on with one another personally, in extended families, in tribal and racial communities, in societies, in nations, and in the relationship with the natural world. Relationships may be good or bad, but their essential power for good or evil is constantly recognizable – in history, in personal life and the flourishing of creation. Let's begin with our relationship with creation.

Creation: the natural world

One of the most exciting intellectual adventures of the last 300 or more years has been the scientific exploration of our natural environment. It is impossible to exaggerate either its interest or the far-reaching nature of its influence. Our knowledge of the world has been changed out of all recognition, and through the development of technology our world has itself changed out of all recognition too. But perhaps even more profoundly, our developing knowledge of the world has led to a transformed view of ourselves. This is the result not only of what we have learned about our world and ourselves and what we can do with our knowledge, but by the very fact that we have been able to think through our discoveries about the world and apply them successfully for our benefit. Humankind has the capacity to enquire about the world intelligently, plan and execute experiments; it seems that we can think about the universe 'from beginning to end' in terms which are becoming increasingly accurate and precise.

So, first, the fundamental forces which hold it together and provide its energy are being opened to enquiry: there are still even some theoretical physicists who entertain the thought that, though not yet within our grasp, it remains within the bounds of possibility that there could be one unified theory which holds together the macro and micro aspect of physical explanation. I happen not to share their confidence, but largely for philosophical, not scientific reasons: I am unclear how one could ever know that one had come to the end of one's enquiring. However far we get, it seems to me that we shall remain curious, puzzled, but keen to understand and in a position to make further progress. But we are trying with some success to work out what it means to talk of the universe having a beginning and an end.

Second, we are making rapid strides in uncovering the genetic code and suitably intrigued to find confirmation that it has a single coherence; all living things are connected by means of DNA, and yet each person's DNA is sufficiently different for it to be almost certainly unique. Professor Watson, of the Crick and Watson partnership that discovered DNA, recently received a prize in honour of his work, a DVD that listed the three billion elements of his personal genetic code. Many developments in pharmaceutical treatments, medical practice and attitudes to disease have followed with surprising speed. We have far to go, but the potential is huge, with some specialists in the field suggesting that human longevity may be extended dramatically over the coming centuries.

With this knowledge, we have transformed the means and speed of transport and communication, pharmaceutics and medical practice, engineering techniques and agriculture. And there is more to come, much more, with developments in bioengineering, nanotechnology, new materials, research into alternative sources of energy, space exploration and the conditions pertaining at the beginning of the universe.

But perhaps the most thrilling aspect of it all is the realization of the capacities of our human brains and what it says about human being: there seems no limit to what we are capable of learning. We are capable of imagining, planning, enquiring, experimenting, discovering, calculating, processing, arguing about and absorbing the information so as to talk about it with one another, build up a picture of our world and our relationship with it, and make use of it. This has crucially transformed our self-awareness. Who are we that we can think all this, do all this, and continue to imagine what more we might do in the future?

This is not achieved on our own, of course: it is not an individual achievement, though there has been, is, and no doubt will continue to be the occasional person whose genius has grasped the significance of a new direction of enquiry or recognized the implications of past work and massively influenced the future. Our knowledge is almost always the product of collaborative experiment in teams, of public conversation among experts and the subsequent delivery of it all into the public domain. As a result of all this we are confident that we know for certain that we have an integral relationship with the material world. It is important to work at what this implies for us and what we do.

Thus, by our behaviour as human beings we learn how to influence the future of our world and of ourselves as part of it. We shall only realize the responsibility we have clearly and accurately, and act properly with the full authority that we possess, if we understand ourselves to be in communion with it. Butterfly wings and all that! We and the world constitute one living sentient reality. The interdependence of ourselves and our world means that we increasingly see ourselves as accountable for its well-being – not, of course, its existence. Our decisions affect it, as they affect us; they increase or limit opportunity just as they extend human choice or limit it. Learning to live well in communion with the world is a key feature of each person's life and of the life of the whole world. It is impossible to think that in death we are alone, apart from the living material of the natural world.

One implication of this is that our souls, in the sense that I have discussed them in the preceding chapter, are not pre-formed 'things' that are thrown into our bodies from outside; there is nothing extra about us. They emerge in our consciousness as we learn about and accept our place in the world. But just as the language we develop to talk about our world with one another is not identical with the world,[93] so neither is the language that incorporates these words. Their use itself raises epistemological and ontological questions. We enjoy a fully embodied life, in communion with a lively natural world of fascinating promise and opportunity.

The story of human institutional life together

We occupy space–time and in so doing share in a variety of histories. Certainly there is the history of the natural world, which we understand in terms of the theory of evolution. But there is in addition the history of the human race, the emergence of structured societies, institutions, communities and nations, of which each of us is in one way or another a member. John Searle has argued that one distinguishing feature of the human race in contrast to the rest of the animal world is that we have organized ourselves by means of institutions.[94] He includes in the set of institutions, families, nation states, sports societies, universities, money, language and the like – the list is huge.

They function, Searle argues, because they have what he calls *deontic* qualities, by which he means that their authority, such as they have, flows from the fact that we agree to attribute it to them, agree to accept it, and act upon it – they do not have it of themselves. Thus while an ant is in a social structure, and bees may even have in their 'dancing' a language in which to indicate the direction of good nectar, they have evolved in that way without conscious thought. For them or processes similar to them to be classified as institutions, they would have had to be intentionally developed. The establishment of the convention of money, and the operation of state bureaucracies, has come about through the intentional activity of human beings who have decided rationally in the light of the evidence to build and develop such institutions.

There are important implications for human self-understanding here too. As human society has evolved and new institutions have emerged, the ways in which persons have thought about themselves, their freedoms and responsibilities, their opportunities and hopes, have evolved too. The self-understanding of the first humans some 50,000 years ago was radically different from that of those who lived in the Stone Age, the Middle Ages, those who lived post-Enlightenment from those who live in the twenty-first century. In order to find out who we are, where we are and learn how to navigate our own way within our human world, it will be necessary – certainly it will be helpful – if we learn to tell the story of the human race, our region, our nation, and indeed our locality. It will be necessary to introduce one another to the ways in which the institution of money operates, and understand the ways in which the legal and educational systems function in our society. Only thus will we have a life that we can live, rather than one that we find is, as it were, lived for us by the zombie-ish role we find ourselves playing.

It is not, however, that we are merely learning objectively about our nation, the institution of money and the operation of the legal system; we are learning to be participant members of the many worlds which we inhabit. If we are not in communion with them, as it were, we shall be out of kilter with one another and struggle as we strive to find ourselves while believing ourselves to be in isolation from others. True communion with our worlds means contributing to them, sharing in their lives so as to develop them and thus make them more responsive to our needs and interests.

Of course, human institutions can run out of steam and collapse, as the Soviet empire did gradually, culminating in the shattering events of 1989. The 'good life' they promised through their collective political, economic and social structures fragmented under pressure from new systems of communication that made knowledge of the wider world more available to more people. The underground rumblings of dissatisfaction burst into the open from time to time; and then irresistibly, as the hopes associated with communism were seen to be illusory in comparison with the freedoms and prosperity of the Western world, the institutions of the communist world were no longer believed uniquely powerful in serving human well-being. They had lost their saltiness and were perceived to be no longer useful. Jesus' words to his disciples made their mark as we can tell, because they are found in all three of the Synoptic Gospels: it is of general application. Salt that has lost its savour is good for nothing but to be thrown away (Matthew 5.13, Mark 9.49, Luke 14.34). But this just illustrates the significance of the communion that we have in and with the various institutions of which we are a part. They do not exist if we lose faith in them and choose to withdraw our support.

Human beings are not simply curious in a static sense ('What is this?'), they are curious in a dynamic sense ('What is going on here?'), in a creative sense ('What can we do to improve things?'), and in an imaginative sense ('How could we conceive of things differently?'). Institutional structures are the forms of life by which we become accountable for the ways in which we understand the world, try to learn more about it, and make it better. Learning to make something of them, to involve ourselves constructively with them – which must include sensible and creative criticism – is part of what we essentially are as human persons.

Indeed, in theological terms, I suggest that in all these ways in which we explore our understanding, care for our physical world and share in the maintenance of our social structures and where appropriate their transformation, we are sharing with God in the redemptive creation of God's world. Institutions have lives, like human beings: this means they have a past and a future, and a 'thick present', which is why revolutions are much less likely to be effective than the drip of gentle evolutionary pressure. Hence historians who try to identify critical moments of change – the Enlightenment, the Industrial Revolution, the origins of the First World War, etc. – are, while certainly interesting, less helpful than those who trace events over the course of a long period. They enable us to enter into the story of our race, economy and intellectual framework so as to be able to tell the story for ourselves and share the life they present.

The moment of truth which a person finds in death sums up all that has been absorbed over a lifetime of participative interaction with the historical traditions of the race as instantiated in the 'thick moment' we present in the fact of dying. Nothing could make plainer the point above in Chapter 2. Learning to die well is a matter of learning to live well. To do this, it is important to realize one's potential as a local focus of the evolution of the natural world, and as a personal focus of the evolution of institutional society.

The world of the arts: landscaping to painting, literature, music, film, theatre and critical writing

The imagination is the root of enquiry in many areas, including the glamorous area of the sciences. Were we not able to picture literally, represent in outline form, or model mathematically what we think we see, we should have no opportunity to modify it, interpret it, experiment with it, or discuss it with others. But at least as important is the imaginative world we conjure up and express in the many various artistic forms. There is not space to allude briefly to more than three of them.

I like to think of the poet as a maker, the builder of worlds public and private, into which we are invited, or which the poet offers as a stimulus not simply of feeling but of thought. Reading, or perhaps more often hearing a poem, can truly be a revelation. John Donne, Coleridge, Thomas Hardy, T. S. Eliot, W. H. Auden, Ezra Pound, Ted Hughes, and of course Shakespeare himself, are just some of the poets that I am driven back to from time to time because their language, insight and personal expression excites me to want to get further into them. They offer not simply an opportunity to re-read what I have previously read, but to gain from renewed acquaintance after a period of other reading and thinking. They sum up a sense of the real world and provide a medium for shared reflection and interest. Coleridge mused often on the nature of poetry and the role of the poet:

> The poet, described in ideal perfection, brings the whole soul of man into activity, with the subordination of its faculties to each other, according to their relative worth and dignity. He diffuses a tone and spirit of unity that blends and (as it were) fuses, each into each, by that synthetic and magical power to which we have exclusively appropriated the name of imagination. This power, first put in action by the will and understanding and retained under their irremissive, though gentle and unnoticed, controul . . . reveals itself in the balance of reconciliation of opposite or discordant qualities: of sameness, with difference, of the general, with the concrete; the idea, with the image; the individual with the representative; the sense of novelty and freshness, with old familiar objects; a more than usual state of emotion, with more than usual order; judgement ever awake and steady self-possession, with enthusiasm and feeling profound or vehement; and while it

blends and harmonizes the natural and the artificial, still sub-ordinates art to nature; the manner to the matter; and our admiration of the poet to our sympathy with the poetry.[95]

To think of the role of the poet in this way is thrilling. The poet is, above all, a maker of meaning; as Coleridge also said, 'The Poet is the man made to solve the riddle of the universe.'

One might do worse, it has often seemed to me, than regard one's life as a poem in which one tries to express everything which one has understood about oneself and the world and one's place in it. To be oneself, of course, one would have also to include some at least of what one had not understood about the world and which one wanted to know. As a maker, any self-respecting poet, and especially Coleridge, will know perfectly well that the making of a work of art is never finished; he just recognizes that he has reached a point when he can do no more. But, as I suggested in the first chapter, there is always time enough to achieve something, to recognize that we have made progress, if not as much as we would have liked.

As the second form I take the novel. Novels come in many shapes and forms. Light fiction is largely without character, disposable and unmemorable: it can usefully if mindlessly fill the boring hours in the departure lounge when your plane is delayed because you have one ear open for announcements, and half your mind on the business of the meeting to which you are going. The last thing such fiction suggests, or indeed is intended to suggest, is that you are reading something to which you will want to return for further insight and refreshment.

But there are many dramatic novels, the reading of which may transform one's sense of what it is to be a lively human being. It is often said that in order to gain the most from a read-ing of a fine novel, we must suspend disbelief: but surely only in one sense. We must allow the author to present in the story another view of the world for our consideration. However, as in any conversation we listen with our mind open, not empty. Indeed, in fact that is the best we can do. But in considering the fictional world of social relationships, moral dispositions, human emotion, human character, in a world as different from our own as the author can manage, we are constantly stimulated to ask new questions and to propose to ourself new answers to old questions.

What does this mean? I can only illustrate it from my own experience. Ahab, in *Moby Dick*, struggles to gain revenge on the white whale that bit off his leg on the assumption, as it were, that if he did not get it, it would finish him.[96] Which provokes the question, what in each of our lives are we pursuing with self-destructive vigour on the false assumption that its elimination will rid our world of all that threatens it? Who, in reading *Birdsong,* has not been led to think through again the morality of war, the suffering of those involved, and the awful position of those whose decisions have made war inevitable?[97] Who could read *The Poisonwood Bible* and not find herself having to reconsider the terrible evil wreaked by the blindness and casual indifference of all forms of fundamentalist doctrine, not excluding Christianity, and the awful impact it has had and is having on societies, individuals and their relationships?[98] The sheer experience of reading them is exhausting.

Of course, it is very often reinvigorating, liberating and encouraging too. To realize that we are all in the same boat, struggling with our anger, resentment and fear, can lead, as it does for Ishmael in *Moby Dick*, to the radical reconsideration of our self-regarding perspective and its rebirth in a public-regarding human perspective, which includes us also. But this is no secondary implication from traditional Christian doctrine, which, inspired by Hawthorne, Melville apparently rejected. The opportunity to 'find ourselves' is implicit in the story itself. There is something worthwhile that we can make of our experience. After reading *Birdsong*, we might reconsider any earlier belief we had had in the just war thesis. How could there be such a thing as a just war, if it committed so many people to drown in mud, and see such impossible ambitions fail in the face of careless action?

In the circumstances pertaining in our time, how now do we think through the issues raised by the possibility of nuclear war, and the inevitable consequences of collateral damage involving innocent civilians? But who are the innocent civilians? Are there any such? The error of fundamentalism is that it makes no room for doubt, let alone error, and seems true by definition to the earnest believer; it is all-consuming. The believer is thought by his belief. This is in total contrast to the view of Christian faith that I hold integral to it, namely that it frees one to make sense of one's experience for oneself. Of course this is not an isolated or private matter, for one relies on others for information, insight and wisdom, and the regular stimulus of the probing question which will set one off again.

In this regard, also the living of a life is like the writing of a novel: both are very dangerous matters. Neither has, it seems to me, a beginning or an end, yet each begins and ends. What I mean by this, is that the narrative of a novel may begin at one point in a character's life, but as the events unfold in the writing, the author finds out more about the subject's past as new events bring into new focus what he had imagined when he began the novel; on reconsideration it turns out to be in need of depth and reinterpretation. And when it comes to the close, it is at least likely that an author will simply find that the narrative has come to an end in an unplanned rather than the original planned manner; many an author has found the novel-ending a surprise.

Hence it is really important to take seriously the reader-response theory in literary criticism. The reader and the author are a partnership exploring a theme through the shared living of a narrative.[99] Without a reading public, there would be no sense in any work of fiction, because there would be no means of discovering, even for the author, what it was all about. The author offers a work to the public in the hope that it has meaning, but the reader in conversation with the text will judge the meaning.

In a way that is worth thinking about, there is an analogy here with a life. The life which I live in exploration of meaning in the light of my understanding of the world, is in its totality, complete or not, offered to God who reads it and helps me make sense of it. The judgement, if it can be so called, is a collaborative enterprise, to which each is committed. What is intriguing, it seems to me, about this analogy is the mutual intention to make it work, to give it meaning. That is what we are concerned to encourage one another to do in the Christian life – to give meaning to our lives in partnership with God, for the world's sake. And the meaning could only become clear at the end, when what we had set out with is clarified in the 'thick moment' of death.

Third, painting gives form to life really and possibly in order to free us from the self-imposed forms with which we surround ourselves. This is one of the most exciting features of art in all its forms, but because it is 'in one's face', painting has a particular tendency to shock, to take one out of one's self. The stylized representation in the conventions of medieval painting shock us by the occasional intrusion of the mouse peeping round the corner of a chair, the slight relaxation in the expression on a saint's face, or the tensed muscle of a proud horse.

When the group around Claude Monet, christened contemptuously 'the Impressionists', had their first exhibition in 1874 in Paris, the world of art was astounded. The artists wanted to paint the effect of light on objects, rather than the objects themselves. Cézanne and the Post-Impressionists were celebrated by Clive Bell; their sense of the world and their relationship with it was focused on form and shape using line and colour to highlight their character. Kandinsky, liberated even more from the world of impressions, was fascinated by colours, their relationships and meaning. While Picasso, dissatisfied with representational art, employed many styles to reveal new dimensions of the world. And where now? The brutal realism of Francis Bacon and the transformations of reality in the 'pickled' forms, and most recently a bejewelled skull called 'The Love of God' by Damien Hurst. Conversation about art can be very confusing. What is art coming to? What are we supposed to get out of it?

And your life? When you look at it, what are you supposed to get out of it? How would you describe it? What does your life represent? What have you made of the materials that you were given? Have you in the history of your world ever changed your style, reconsidered your perspective, and developed the perspective that you live in? The analogy is loose but significant, I think. We are neither constricted in our perspective, nor free from limitations. The canvas on which we paint is of limited perspective, but the colours and forms that we explore are virtually infinite. What will God see when he takes the wrapping off our gift of ourselves in death?

Liberation to enquire, to explore our worlds and to inhabit them, to express ourselves in them is what we are promised in Christian faith. As in art, the search is not self-contained or lonely, but always in the light of what others have imaginatively succeeded in creating. Our lives are made in the company of others, and the gift that we are making is made in the light of the totality of the experience that we have gathered and from which we are made. To establish communion with all such searching is itself an art that informs and encourages our own imaginative exploration and achievements. Becoming ourselves is a joint enterprise with all who aspire to love God and God's world.

The worlds of meaning and purpose

In an earlier book, I said that I doubted whether the person had yet been born who was not puzzled about life and wanted to explore the question of its purpose and meaning.[100] I am still in doubt, though it is true I have met a few people who claim that since there is no answer it is not a real question and therefore they try not to waste their time thinking about it. However, for most of us the question of life's meaning is one we have from time to time explored. It is certainly something which one associates with mortality. Can there have been any point in my life, as I contemplate its insignificance, its mistakes and failures, even its modest successes and satisfactions? Have I anything to show for it?

There are many traditions, largely but by no means exclusively of a religious character, that purport to offer a meaningful account of human being. A unique feature of the Christian faith in its essence is that it talks of faith, never certainty. Indeed, as opposed to some traditions of religious believing, even some mistaken interpretations of the Christian faith, we recognize certainty as inimical to faith, not doubt. How can one grow in understanding, when one believes that what one 'knows' is all that there is to know or all one needs to know?

Like the majority of the human race, Christians work with a world that they believe is within their grasp, but which they recognize to be beyond their control. Thus, while we may not know the details of the meaning and purpose implicit in our experience of the world, we are free to make something of it, and believe that it is meaningful. In death, we die with the living hope that the gift we offer will continue to contribute to the revealing of the truth; and that God will make sense of our gift for the world's well-being.

The Communion of Saints

In Christian theology we express this truth in terms of the imagery summoned up by the doctrine of the Communion of Saints. This is the Body of Christ, which is aware of Christ's presence, and enjoys sharing in the work to which he was called by God the Father, to reveal his love in creation. It embraces all people, from every generation under the sun who have wanted God and sought him in their lives. The demands of love are such that one can never know the outcome for certain, but the vision of its real possibility is such that one is not discouraged.

Christ's Body is in principle the Church, the total community of faith and affection into which we are incorporated in baptism, and to which we belong in the whole of our faithful lives. It is, Christ reminds us in every celebration of the Eucharist, the community that has the responsibility of living out the implications of his presence; that is, it is to express in its life here and now the fact of God's love for God's creation. The point is that in death, we die still surrounded by this company of faithful witnesses, and therefore also in the presence of Christ. Far from being alone, we die in the faith, with the offering of the little that we have made on our lives given all of which we are a part, for the greater glory of God and the renewal of God's world.

Pope John XXIII towards the end of his life began his spiritual testament with these words:

> On the point of presenting myself before the Lord, One and Three, who created me, redeemed me, chose me to be priest and Bishop and bestowed graces upon me, I entrust my poor soul to his mercy. Humbly I beg his pardon for my sins and failings; I offer him what little good, even if imperfect and unworthy, I was able with his help to do for his glory and in the service of Holy Church and for the edification of my fellows, and I implore him finally to welcome me, like a kind and tender father, among the saints in the bliss of eternity.[101]

Perhaps we are neither priest nor Bishop; perhaps we have not had Angelo Roncalli's opportunities to serve; but each of us is, as he is, a soul. Each of us has something to give as we contemplate the whole of our lives. Each of us, as a Christian, will want our offering of ourselves in death to be accepted in the community of the faithful. Each of us in this sense dies with the world, God's creation, in the presence of God in faith and hope. At last we have responded to the immortal words made famous by Mae West (but originally spoken by God?), 'Come up and see me sometime.' We yearn to have the confidence to say 'Sure', when the time comes.

> Jesus, lover of my soul,
>   Let me to thy bosom fly,
> While the nearer waters roll,
>   While the tempest still is nigh;
> Hide me, O my Saviour, hide,
>   Till the storm of life is past;
> Safe into the haven guide,
>   O receive my soul at last![102]

What we 'say' and express in death is our summation of the world's life with God, what we have made of our lives with others, the meaning we have given to it in the light of the faith we have tried to 'live out'. It is a daring, risky thing that we do, but we do it in faith that our prayer will be heard because God is, we believe, attentive to the world's cry. God's attention to the world involves the giving of God's whole self to the world in selfless concern for the other. In response to this, we make our own offering of the world in ourselves.

7

Death and the Funeral Rites

The mystery of death

For the Christian, life is the symbol of the real presence of God with God's people in God's world. But life includes death, as Meister Eckhardt and Rilke, from their different but overlapping perspectives, saw with utter clarity. Hence in death, when a person gathers up the wholeness of life in one single offering, the Christian funeral rite provides the Community of Faith with the opportunity to celebrate both the offering by the deceased person and the offering of the world's wholeness as enjoyed redemptively in God's good creation.

It is hard for our European Western society to keep this in perspective. We have other preoccupations focused upon extending life, rather than coming to terms with the fact that we have to learn to live with dying and death. And anyway we like to think of ourselves as enlightened; we want to take in our stride the implications of our rational scientific culture with all that it offers. Religion, philosophy and moral considerations are private matters of no real public significance. As the popular American philosopher Richard Rorty said, 'I argue that there are no transcendent answers. Each of us must reach our own conclusions about life, and try to respect the differences among us.'[103] There is a great deal of sympathy with Kant, who in the eighteenth century put it crisply like this:

> Our age is, in especial degree, the age of criticism, and to criticism everything must submit. Religion through its sanctity, and law-giving through its majesty, may seek to exempt themselves from it. But they then awaken just suspicion, and

cannot claim the sincere respect which reason accords only to that which has been able to sustain the test of free and open examination.[104]

This might well be said to sum up our present situation: nothing should be accepted that cannot be proved consistent with reason. The exact implications of this are a matter of continuing debate, but certainly neither religion nor the law can claim exemption from free and open examination. Only by these means can we refine our understanding of the role and nature of religion and identify what is valuable and life-giving from the dross that is born of ignorance and the product of fear. The history of religion is no more of a piece than is that of mathematics or science; there is tripe as well as gold in 'them there hills'. However, I have argued elsewhere that at its best orthodox Christian theological enquiry is an essential partner in the public conversation about the qualities of reasonable discourse, meaning, purpose and value of life. Theology and religious faith are facets of the generous quality of rational enquiry that respects every aspect of human experience and grounds the truthfulness of judgement in lively conversation. So I agree with Johan Heinrich Merck who wrote not long after Kant:

> Now we have got the freedom of believing in public nothing but what can be rationally demonstrated. They have deprived religion of all its sensuous elements, that is, of all its relish. They have carved it up into its parts and reduced it to a skeleton without colour and light . . . and now it's put in a jar and nobody wants to taste it.[105]

To dissect theological enquiry and religion in such a way that it cannot be seen in any of its forms in its wholeness is to lose contact with one of the ways in which humankind has sought to make sense of human nature. The consideration of death and dying which I have outlined in this book has emphasized their oneness with life when that is placed in the whole framework of thought provided by the recognition of God's commitment of God's self to the well-being of all creation.

As far as we know, humankind has throughout history respected the body of the deceased and wanted to treat it with dignity, even in the absence of a belief in a life after death. There is little evidence, if any, of indifference to the treatment of a deceased's body. The scandal in Liverpool that occurred after the removal of body parts from the cadavers of children without parents' permission, and the unresolved despair of the bereaved when after murder or accidental death by drowning there is no body to bury, both illustrate the point. All traditions, including the humanist, make something of the occasion of a funeral; the Christian most certainly is entitled to do so.

But inevitably the occasion of a funeral brings us face to face all over again with the harsh reality of death and raises the serious question of whether life signifies anything. Does life itself include death, and if so what does it mean for our understanding of the world? The very naturalness of death is encouraging for the Christian. Each person's existence, the Christian says, includes in its finitude a gospel-wholeness and completeness that is more than can be described in literal, empirical terms. A person's death is something to be valued and remembered and celebrated: the funeral is an occasion when we are invited to 'taste and see that the Lord is good', for 'happy are those who take refuge in him'.[106] It is an occasion to be enjoyed, if that does not sound utterly ridiculous – and it should not! – while at the same time recognizing the natural grief and despair that are the concomitant emotions with which death is surrounded. Certainly this anxiety about the nature and meaning of life is consistent with the confident hope with which every Christian funeral service is celebrated.

The very first words spoken by the priest as he precedes the coffin into the church are words of encouragement that resonate with both our fears and our hopes:

'I am the resurrection and the life', says the Lord. 'Those who believe in me, even though they die, will live, and everyone who lives and believes in me will never die.[107]

Their context is significant. According to the Gospel of St John, these are words of Jesus to Martha.[108] Jesus had learned of the death of Lazarus, the brother of Mary and Martha, and determined to travel down into Judea, territory where misunderstandings of what he had said had already led to threats on his life. When the disciples heard of it they were concerned for their own safety, but Thomas, interestingly he of the doubting mind, encouraged them to accompany him even if it meant their own death. Jesus himself, according to John, said that he was glad he was not there when Lazarus died because it gave him an opportunity to encourage their faith. All this is in the context of events where those whom he met failed to 'see' him in his true light. It seems that Jesus, at this moment, felt that in the presence of death the disciples might at last discern God's presence with him, with them, and with God's whole creation.

The whole passage is mysterious; it seems to be an attempt by the evangelist John in the very ordinary situation of death to get at what he believes to be the implicit truth of Christ's presence. I do not know what you make of the story of the raising of Lazarus. If it is a case of the literal restoration to life, the revivification of a person who has died a natural death, then the earlier reference in the chapter to sleep may hold the clue; certainly it seems the most reasonable approach. Lazarus was very ill; they thought he was dead and so he was buried in a cave tomb where the temperature was so low that it kept his body in a state of suspended animation. But Jesus asked to see the body, and when he spoke to him, Lazarus recognized the voice of his old friend and was restored to health.

Stranger things happen. It is reported that in June 2007 Mr Grzebski, a Polish citizen, recovered and spoke to his wife after an accident in a railway marshalling yard had put him in a coma for 19 years. At least this is what was believed until recently, when, as a result of treatment it became apparent that although Mr Grzebski appeared to be in a coma, he was actually conscious and had been suffering from a particular form of aphasia: Lazarus was only in the tomb for four days! However, this reductionist explanation does not seem to fit the character of the story if looked at from the whole point of view of the Gospel.

In the Gospel of John it is not the resurrection that reveals God's glory – that is the sign of God's presence – but the death of Jesus, God incarnate, on the cross: it is Jesus' utter commitment of himself to the world's well-being that makes plain God's eternal loving presence with all his people. It appears that this is what John wants us to see here, and what just possibly Jesus also had in mind. Hence the chapter ends with Jesus withdrawing from public view in order to avoid misunderstanding and to prepare for his move towards Jerusalem, and the whispered discussion among the chief priests and Pharisees regarding their fear that Jesus might risk coming to the Passover festival. We know that Jesus had every intention of doing this, as, of course, every good Jew should.

Thus Jesus, far from having withdrawn from the scene, though this is all the world can see, especially at this moment, affirms the reality of life notwithstanding death by pointing to what he himself will experience. Christ's presence is life-giving and John uses the occasion of Lazarus' death and the grief surrounding it to point forward to the significance of Christ's death for the future of Christian faith and the salvation of the whole world of creation.

Funeral rites

A Christian funeral service takes different forms, whether it is in the home, in church or at the cemetery, or, as may be the case with Anglican and Protestant funerals, at the crematorium. It is usually in three parts, comprising comfort, proclamation and commendation. (I shall want to refer later to the fact that in the Catholic tradition, if the service takes place in church there will also be a celebration of the Eucharist.)

Given the divine–human framework of our lives, we need to put the Christian funeral rite into perspective by looking at the way in which a lifetime's participation in the liturgical practice of the Church encourages faith, hope and charity. To be regularly reminded of the eternal benefits that flow from faith in Christ when one worships with the Church, especially when one shares in the sacramental celebration of Christ's death and passion, cultivates a readiness for death.

A lifetime's faithful practice is a marvellous privilege, but one must never forget that a person may indeed accept God at the last, even in the course of dying, as did the penitent thief crucified with our Lord. The story, for example, that Shakespeare reaffirmed his likely Catholic upbringing at his death is very possibly true.[109] On the other hand, the story that circulated in some Catholic circles in North Wales after the death of Bertrand Russell to the effect that he was reconciled with God at the end through the ministry of a local priest is almost certainly untrue.[110] But to be part of a living tradition with its stories, sacraments, regular set of pointers, reminders, encouragements and hopes is the best possible preparation for the offering which one makes of one's life in dying. It makes plain that at the end one is supported by the whole Church.

The sacramental economy of the celebration of the Living Christ in the Church, launched by the outpouring of the Spirit at Pentecost, confirms and expresses the reality of God's gracious presence in the divinely human nature of our world. One begins to share in it when one is baptized, and continues until death in the regular celebration of the Eucharist, variously called the Mass, the Holy Communion, the Lord's Supper. These two sacraments are celebrated in (almost) all traditions of the Christian Church. With them are included, in the Roman Catholic and Orthodox traditions, confirmation, penance, anointing of the sick, ordination and marriage.[111] All are lively symbols of the gift of salvation, offered to all people by God the Father through the Son in the Holy Spirit. All of them bear testimony to God's healing presence: hence the appropriateness of the title 'physician' often given to Christ. He is associated with healing miracles in the New Testament, but above all with the forgiveness of sin, the bringing together of a person's physical, moral, social, private and public life, into the wholeness of personhood in the presence of God, to which in the Christian tradition we give the name 'soul'.

The Anointing of the Sick is a rare sacrament in Protestantism and Anglicanism; indeed it is, I'm told, sadly becoming less frequent in the Roman Catholic Church. Protestants and Anglicans more usually offer prayers with and for those who are sick, often in the intercessions of the Eucharist. However, an insight into the theology associated with the sacrament is helpful. It especially focuses the role of Christ in the Church in bringing health, both physical and spiritual, to the world.

Indeed, in a profound sense, all the sacraments are associated with health and healing; the Anointing of the Sick simply focuses that association at the time of a person's special need in time of ill health. The minister or priest prays with the person for a restoration to health and anoints with oil which has been blessed at the Eucharist on Holy Thursday, thus identifying the whole sacrament with the mystery of Christ's sacrifice. This is no invocation of magical powers; neither is there anything here of faith-healing – whatever that amounts to: rather it celebrates the normality of health for all God's people, despite the present evidence of sickness. Historically, the sacrament of the Anointing of the Sick, also known as unction, was often associated with a celebration of the Eucharist, which further emphasizes its grounding in the Gospel.

Of course, illness is a reminder of mortality, very particularly so in previous centuries when the understanding of the human body and the influences upon it that can bring about its demise were so little understood. It still is for those who have eyes to see. Hence the anointing with oil in the context of sickness as an encouraging sacramental sign of God's presence, available throughout life, came gradually to be especially associated with the process of dying itself and the anticipation of the health of eternal life. But, it seems to me, its link with one's own and the Church's 'management' of one's dying is very moving and illuminating.

Ideally, the Church's recognition of the process of dying will have three dimensions, including the formal summary of a healthful life represented by penance, the prayers for health in anointing with oil (extreme unction) and the viaticum, the last celebration of the Eucharist with all the faithful, including those whose society one still enjoys here and now, and those whose society one anticipates. Not all traditions use these terms, but all in principle take account of their significance in the way in which they approach death. A person makes peace with God and the world, preferably helped by a priest who will if appropriate offer formally the sacrament of penance, the anointing of the sick or the saying of prayers for health, and the celebration of the Eucharist. What better experience of dying could we possibly hope for than one in which we are reminded of the forgiving, healing and risen presence of Christ, accompanied by the whole company of Christ's Church in heaven and on earth in God's good creation!

The funeral service

The funeral service is not itself a sacrament because in dying the deceased has passed beyond the sacramental life. Hence the four parts of the funeral service offer (different in form whether at home, in church or at the cemetery/crematorium) comfort, preaching and celebration of the gospel and commendation of the soul into the hands of God the Father. It is the culmination of a life in Christ initiated in baptism, yet not necessarily the ultimate fulfilment of the divine will in the life of the person who has died.

A procession begins the service. The ceremonial carrying of the coffin into the church, to the cemetery or crematorium, itself symbolizes the nature of the offering that we are making. Here, we seem to be saying, is what this person and we have made and are making of the world God has made. The priest or minister precedes the coffin and the mourners, leading like a shepherd the sheep of Christ's flock.[112] There follows the Ministry of the Word, which includes both the proclamation of the Gospel in familiar readings from scripture, and a sermon.

Too frequently the sermon will take the form of an encomium for the deceased that seems to me entirely inappropriate; if there is to be such a thing then that should in my opinion be confined to a memorial service if such is desired – a quite independent and separate event much later. Of course, it is right simply to express thankfulness for the gift of the deceased's life and all that we have enjoyed and known through the person's friendship and society. However, the real purpose of the proclamation is to set death within the vital framework of the whole Christian gospel. In this way the preacher provides support for believers, reminds those who may be present but who only rarely share in the liturgy of the mystery of faith, and informs those not of the faith who may be there as friends or relations of the deceased. It is or should be a very special occasion and demands much thought both in preparation and in delivery.

Precisely because of the mysterious nature of the occasion and the eternal hope that it represents, it should be down to earth, brief, matter of fact and simple. But both preacher and mourners will find inspiration in the texts themselves.

Even though I walk through the darkest valley,
I fear no evil;
for you are with me;
your rod and your staff –
they comfort me.[113]

Jesus said: I am the bread of life. Whoever comes to me will never be hungry, and whoever believes in me will never be thirsty. But I said to you that you have seen me and yet do not believe. Everything that the Father gives me will come to me, and anyone who comes to me I will never drive away; for I have come down from heaven, not to do my own will, but the will of him who sent me. And this is the will of him who sent me, that I should lose nothing of all that he has given me, but raise it up, at the last day. This is indeed the will of my Father, that all who see the Son and believe in him may have eternal life; and I will raise them up on the last day.[114]

Peace I leave with you; my peace I give to you. I do not give to you as the world gives. Do not let your hearts be troubled, and do not let them be afraid.[115]

Protected by the royal power of the Shepherd with his careful attention to my health reminds me of the carefree times of my youth when I used happily to lie down in the grassy meadow and look up at the sky in wonder. Nourished in life by the eternal food of the gospel provided through the Christ whose giving of himself revealed the living presence of God with his people, I now, with all the people of faith, live and die in the confident hope of salvation. We can all, every one of us, enjoy the peace that Christ gives, because it is an extension to us through the Spirit of the peace that the Son knows with the Father.

Within this proclamation there is rightly gathered up the prayers of all present. We pray for ourselves, for all who grieve, for all those to whose salvation Christ's death points; and we do so in full knowledge that we stand in Christ within the fellowship of the Communion of Saints.

The commendation is the only part of the service that is directly concerned with the soul of the deceased and his or her new life. The utter reality of what we are doing is recognized in the words we use:

Into your keeping, O merciful God,
We commend your servant N.
Receive *her/him* into the arms of your mercy,
Into the joy of everlasting peace,
And into the glorious company of the saints in light;
Through Christ our Lord. **Amen**

The person has passed beyond our care and we can do no more than commend him or her to God, that is to entrust his or her soul to the only person in a position now to do anything for them, namely God, the Father, Creator, Redeemer and Sustainer of all that is. Such trustful commendation is, on the other hand, not simply the expression of concern on the part of those present at the funeral but of the whole Community of Faith. It is not the members of the congregation present at the funeral service that alone commends the soul of the departed to God, but the whole Church. There is more to it, however, for it is important to recognize that when I say that the deceased has passed beyond our care this does not mean that he or she has passed beyond our love and therefore our prayers. Indeed, far from it: the departed and we who are present are joined in the common prayer of the Church for evermore.

Eucharistic celebration?

The Roman Catholic Church accompanies the funeral service in the third part, if it is held in church, with a celebration of the Eucharist. This seems to me to be right: I wish it were so more generally throughout the Christian community. It seems most appropriate to me that, especially on the occasion of a funeral, which is not itself a sacrament, the congregation should remember and share in the celebration of the whole faith of the Church.[116] Christ, the One Celebrant of God's gracious presence with God's people in God's world, affirms with the One, Holy, Catholic and Apostolic Church that he called into existence, the loving truth expressed in his own death. Hence, then and now and for ever we continue to pray with him *his* prayer which is now *our* prayer, '*Our* Father'. The praying of this prayer makes present to the supplicant in the most remarkable way the sense of the common life we enjoy when we pray in Christ with the deceased and with all the faithful in the Communion of Saints the prayer of our Lord, the '*Our* Father'. It is life-affirming, nourishing, and a felt testimony to the hope that is within us.

Symbols of light and the cross

There are many symbols associated with the Christian life, some of which have particular significance in the time of death. I mention but two, the lighting of a candle and the sign of the cross. The image of passing from darkness to light is itself a parable of the movement of life in Christ. In the Western Church, the first Eucharist of Easter, celebrated at midnight on Easter Day, begins in the dark with the procession into the church of a lighted candle that is used to light the Paschal Candle from which are lighted all the other candles carried by the congregation. The light of Christ is spread throughout the church. In many churches, at the end of the Easter Season, the Paschal Candle is removed to the baptistry; at each baptism, a candle is lit from the Paschal Candle and given to the father of the baptized as a sign of the child's movement from darkness to light. This sign is present too at a funeral, where a lighted candle symbolizes the prayers of the Church and the faith of the deceased that rise to God in new life.

The sign of the cross marks the sharing of all the faithful in the dying and rising of Christ, which itself is the grounding of the sacrament of baptism. Hence traditionally the dying person would hold a cross – perhaps one from the Palm Sunday celebration, or make the sign of the cross. Certainly it is a dimension of every Christian funeral service, which takes place in the confidence of the merits and grace that flow from the death and resurrection of Christ.

Kant wrote, 'Out of the crooked timber of humanity, nothing straight was ever fashioned.' That may be so if we consider our humanity from a purely human perspective. However, in the divinely human environment in which we live and love and have our being, we can be confident that God does and has in Christ. And it is in God alone – Father, Son and Holy Ghost – that we put our trust.

Such reflections as I have undertaken in writing this book naturally raise questions for me. How do I think of my own death and dying? If I am conscious at the time of my death and not drugged beyond all sensibility, I would like to think that I shall recall to mind the Trinity and be able simply to be thankful, and above all to be grateful to God for my life, my family, the Church and God's good world, and commend them to God. I hope I will remember and be able to pray, as at other times of sickness in life, the *Anima Christi*:

Soul of Christ, sanctify me;
Body of Christ, save me;

Blood of Christ, refresh me;
Water from the side of Christ, wash me;
Passion of Christ, strengthen me;
O good Jesu, hear me;
Within thy wound hide me;
Suffer me not to be separated from thee;
From the malicious enemy defend me;
In the hour of my death call me
And bid me come to thee;
That with the saints I may praise thee
For all eternity. Amen.

And it would be a mercy if I could overhear someone praying the *Proficiscere*, which originated in the Frankish Benedictine Community and which can probably be dated to the second half of the eighth century.[117] The inclusiveness of this prayer of commendation associates the soul of the deceased with the liberation of the souls of all faithful people. The first part of it is familiar to all in the words of John Henry Newman, set to some of the most triumphant of Elgar's music in *The Dream of Gerontius*:

Proficiscere, anima Christiana, de hoc mundo!
Go forth upon thy journey, Christian soul!
Go from this world! Go in the name of God
The Omnipotent Father, Who created thee!
Go, in the name of Jesus Christ, our Lord,
Son of the living God, Who bled for thee!
Go, in the name of the Holy Spirit,
Who hath been poured out on thee! Go in the name
Of Angels and Archangels; in the name
Of Thrones and Dominations; in the name
Of Princedoms and of Powers; and in the name
Of Cherubim and Seraphim, go forth!

Go, in the name of Patriarchs and Prophets;
And of Apostles amd Evangelists,
Of Martyrs and Confessors, in the name

Of holy Monks and Hermits; in the name
Of holy Virgins; and all the Saints of God,

Both men and women, go! Go on thy course!
And may thy place today be found in peace,
And may thy dwelling be the Holy Mount
     Of Sion – through the same, through Jesus Christ our Lord.

And if I have the strength I shall hope to pray the '*Our* Father'.

Epilogue

The Experience of Death
in Poetry and Music

This chapter consists of some readings, music and pictures – even a whole book – which I find encouraging: they open vistas that give me pause for thought and stimulate positive reflection. Of course, readers will want to add from their own store of shared experience and I would encourage them to do so. I take it for granted that the Bible, a hymnbook and the liturgy will provide inspiration through their regular use: even the most familiar lines can strike one anew. They should be allowed to do so.

I

Tennyson wrote *In Memoriam A.H.H.* between 1830 and 1850 in memory of his friend Arthur Hallam who died suddenly in Vienna aged 22. These stanzas written in 1849 were the introduction to the first publication. The strong faith that many find in *In Memoriam* was questioned by T. S. Eliot who in 1936 commented that '*In Memoriam* is a poem of despair, but of despair of a religious kind.'[118] In view of Tennyson's thoughtful, lifelong concern with immortality, this must be right. But it therefore offers a realistic hope that can be set within the framework explored in this book.

Strong Son of God, Immortal Love,
    Whom we, that have not seen thy face,
    By faith, and faith alone, embrace,
Believing where we cannot prove;

Thine are these orbs of light and shade;
 Thou madest Life in man and brute;
 Thou madest Death; and lo, thy foot
Is on the skull which thou hast made.

Thou wilt not leave us in the dust:
 Thou madest man, he knows not why,
 He thinks he was not made to die;
And thou hast made him: thou art just.

Thou seemest human and divine,
 The highest, holiest manhood, thou:
 Our wills are ours, we know not how;
Our wills are ours, to make them thine.

Our little systems have their day;
 They had their day and cease to be:
 They are but broken lights of thee,
And thou, O Lord, art more than they.

We have but faith: we cannot know;
 For knowledge is of things we see
 And yet we trust it comes from thee,
A beam in darkness: let it grow.

Let knowledge grow from more to more,
 But more of reverence in us dwell;
 That mind and soul, according well,
May make one music as before,

But vaster. We are fools and slight;
 We mock thee when we do not fear:
 But help thy foolish ones to bear;
Help thy vain worlds to bear thy light.

Forgive what seem'd my sin in me;
 What seem'd my worth since I began;

For merit lives from man to man,
And not from man, O Lord, to thee.

Forgive my grief for one removed,
   Thy creature, whom I found so fair,
   I trust he lives in thee, and there
I find him worthier to be loved.

Forgive these wild and wandering cries,
   Confusions of a wasted youth;
   Forgive them where they fail in truth,
And in thy wisdom make me wise.

II

Edward Elgar's *Dream of Gerontius* sets words of John Henry
Newman published in 1860 some 20 years after he abandoned the
Church of England and became a Roman Catholic. Newman's
bold words combined with the sensitive force of Elgar's music are
to my mind absolutely thrilling. Every now and again it does one
good to hear the directness of the words with which Gerontius
addresses Jesus and Mary, the gentle concern of the priest, the
praises of the Angelic Host, and the angel's assurance that salvation is promised through the mercy of God. *Proficiscere, anima
Christiana, de hoc mundo* – 'Go forth Christian soul'. What an
invitation! 'Praise to the holiest in the height!' Yes, indeed!

III

Franz Schubert (1797–1828), *Winterreise*, 1827

There is no composer of lieder to surpass Schubert: the *Winterreise*
is his greatest achievement. It is a setting of 24 poems by the
Dresden poet Wilhelm Müller in which Schubert exactly cap-
tures the Romantic association of love with death. But the vision

of the individual songs and of the cycle as a whole expresses the profound luminescence of the eternity of love. The songs do not tell a story; the cycle is a collection of life experiences expressed by creative intelligence and the sensitivity of the human voice. Schubert never sets words to music; he translates the words *into* music, he 'says' the words in music.

There are many CD versions available. Dietrich Fischer-Dieskau with Gerald Moore, Matthias Goerne with Alfred Brendel or Peter Pears with Benjamin Britten offer distinctive and beautiful accounts. Any will reward repeated listening.

IV

When it comes to painting we seem unwilling to give the time to it that will bring it alive and free it to feed our souls. We walk around an exhibition so swiftly that we are unable to establish a relationship with any picture or piece of sculpture – sometimes indeed we have to when it is very popular and we are taken around by the crowd rather than making our own progress. From 26 February to 7 May 2000 the National Gallery put on an exhibition called 'Seeing Salvation'. The excellent catalogue was called *The Image of Christ*, which the Yale University Press distributed. Look at the catalogue or, if you can, purchase one for yourself. It will pay dividends if you work through the book slowly, giving proper attention to each painting. You may not like them all; indeed their violence can often offend our contemporary sensitivities, yet there is not one from which we cannot gain insight and learn hope, as we trace the feelings of Christians through the ages as they try to express the inexpressible in their art. A very high proportion of the pictures comes from British collections, most from the National Gallery itself, and so there is the added advantage that one can see the originals for oneself and spend time with them. If you happen to be unfamiliar with the genre, *Painting the Word*, a delightfully informative book by John Drury (Yale University Press, 1999) is the ideal companion.

V

Thomas Hardy (1840–1928), 'The Darkling Thrush'

Thomas Hardy, very widely read for his novels, wanted above all to be known as a poet. His reputation continues to grow. He protested in his novels at the injustice of life and mourned the passing of the communities of human society which 'commercialization' was beginning to bring about. His poetry can likewise be regarded as dismal, even morbid, yet that is to misunderstand it. He found in the events of the natural world an awakening to reconsider possibilities that his life experiences had pushed aside. This poem identifies such a potentially awakening moment. It is vital to keep one's ear open for such thrilling sounds.

I leant upon a coppice gate
   When Frost was spectre-gray
And Winter's dregs made desolate
   The weakening eye of day.
The tangled bine-stems scored the sky
   Like strings of broken lyres,
And all mankind that haunted nigh
   Had sought their household fires.

The land's sharp features seemed to be
   The Century's corpse outleant,
His crypt the cloudy canopy,
   The wind his death-lament.
The ancient pulse of germ and birth
   Was shrunken hard and dry,
And every spirit upon earth
   Seemed fervourless as I.

At once a voice arose among
   The bleak twigs overhead
In a full-hearted evensong

Of joy illimited;
An aged thrush, frail, gaunt, and small,
  In blast-beruffled plume,
Had chosen thus to fling his soul
  Upon the growing gloom.

So little cause for carollings
  Of such ecstatic sound
Was written on terrestrial things
  Afar or nigh around,
That I could think there trembled through
  His happy good-nigh air
Some blessed Hope, whereof he knew
  And I was unaware.

(Thomas Hardy, *Collected Poems*, London,
Macmillan, 1952, p. 137)

VI

Ezra Pound (1885–1972) was a curious mixture of genius and confusion, but his poetry is never anything but intriguing. His celebration for a friend is personal and powerful. Death may appear to have the last word, but it is not all-conquering.

For E. McC.

That was my counter-blade under Leonardo Terrone, Master of Fence

Gone while your tastes were keen to you,
Gone where the grey winds call to you,
By that high fencer, even Death,
Struck by the blade that no man parrieth;
Such is your fence, one saith,
  One that hath known you.
Drew you your sword most gallantly
Made you your pass most valiantly
  'Gainst that grey fencer, even Death.

Gone as a gust of breath
Faith! No man tarrieth,
'*Se il cor to manca*', but it failed thee not!
'*Non to fidar*', it is the sword that speaks
'*In me.*'[119]

Thou trusted'st in thyself and met the blade
'Thout mask or gauntlet, and art laid
As memorable broken blades that be
Kept as bold trophies of old pageantry.
As old Toledos past their days of war
Are kept mnemonic of the strokes they bore,
So art thou with us, being good to keep
In your heart's sword-rack, thou thy sword-arm sleen.

ENVOIE

Struck by the blade that no man parrieth,
Pierced of the point that toucheth lastly all,
'Gainst that grey fencer, even Death,
Behold the shield! He shall not take thee all.

(Ezra Pound, *Selected Poems*, introduced by T. S. Eliot, London,
Faber & Faber, 1928, pp. 46–7)

VII

Pablo Neruda (1904–73) was a Chilean diplomat, politician, member of the Communist Party and a supporter of Allende; in 1971 he won the Nobel Prize for Literature. He wrote a large number of beautiful love poems: many have been set to music. Peter Lieberson set five poems from Neruda's *100 Love Sonnets* for his wife, the mezzo-soprano Lorraine Hunt Lieberson. She recorded them live with the Boston Symphony Orchestra on 25–26 November 2005, when they already knew that she was mortally ill with cancer: she died the following year. To hear them now with that knowledge I find almost unbearable, but

perhaps for that very reason, revelatory. After all, if we are serious, the parting in death is, as Neruda frequently proclaims, not
the end of love.

Sonnet XCII

My love, if I die and you don't –,
My love, if you die and I don't –,
Let's not give grief an even greater field.
No expanse is greater than where we live.

Dust in the wheat, sand in the deserts,
Time, wandering water, the vague wind
Swept us on like sailing seeds.
We might have found one another in time.

This meadow where we find ourselves.
O little infinity! We give it back.
But, Love, this love has not ended:

Just as it never had a birth, it has
No death, it is like a river,
Only changing lands, and changing lips.

(trans. Stephen Tapscott)

VIII

There are two musical compositions that create time and space
in which to think when I listen to them. Olivier Messiaen (1908–
92), *Quartet for the End of Time* (1941) and Heinrich Ignaz
Franz von Biber (1644–1704), *The Mystery Sonatas*.

Messiaen's Catholic faith inspired him to attempt to incarnate
the mysterious sense of the divine in music. This was never more
so than in *Quatuor pour la fin du Temps*. He wrote it when a
German prisoner of war in Silesia. He had somehow brought
with him a writing instrument and some manuscript paper: the
instrumentation was determined by the fact that there were with
him three musicians, a violinist and a clarinetist who had their

instruments with them, and a cellist. The latter had no instrument though his captors procured one for him, albeit one with only three strings. An ancient out-of-tune piano was brought in for Messiaen to play – in the cold of Stalag VIII A – at the first performance on 15 January 1941. The whole work is a triumph of hope over adversity: I cannot hear it without being aware of the stark warmth of the composition in the desolate cold of imprisonment. There is nothing but freedom here; no limitation can frustrate the human imagination and its capacity to create. There are many recordings.

Heinrich Biber was the greatest violinist of the seventeenth century and almost as famous in his time as a composer. He was a member of the *Kapelle* of the Archbishop of Salzburg, becoming Kapellmeister in 1684. Interest in his compositions has recently grown, most especially for these sonatas that are meditations on biblical scenes as found in the Rosary: the *Five Sorrowful Mysteries*, *Five Joyful Mysteries*, *Five Glorious Mysteries*. Each is pervaded by a quiet, bold confidence. The recording by John Holloway, David Moroney and Tragicomedia is two CDs on Virgin Veritas.

IX

Thomas Blackburn (1916–77), 'Dialogue'

Thomas Blackburn, a lecturer in English, wrote nine books of poetry. His work is a disciplined exploration of the human soul whose search for truth in the face of shame finds no rest in himself, only the possibility of new ventures through acceptance and fellowship in the human–divine dimension.

Dialogue

Where are you going to my fellow, my friend
Ash on your hair and black is your dress?
I go to a garden to ask for pardon
That I fled flying from in my distress.

And where is that garden my friend, my fellow?
That garden of grief I indeed wish to see.
Then draw your heart's curtain and it is certain
You will find the place called Gethsemane.

I know that name my fellow, my friend,
It's the apex of sadness why are you not sad?
I am sick of flying and wish for dying
And I'm going to meet the son of a God.

But what will die there, my fellow, my friend?
And why this relief when there should be grief?
I will die to that entity, the smallness of me
And in uncircumscribed being, follow living.

Then may I go with you my friend, my fellow?
I also am tired of my groping ego.
By accepting pain, pain will change if not go,
So follow me then friend, my fellow follow.

(Thomas Blackburn, *Post Mortem*, Liverpool,
Rondo Publications Ltd, 1977, p. 39)

X

Eugenio Montale (1896–1981), 'The Lemons'

Eugenio Montale, poet, prose writer, artist and journalist, lived
in Italy all his life. He was occasionally in danger because his
poetry was regarded by some as criticism of fascism: it may well
have been. Certainly the limpid discernment in his consideration
of ordinary things refuses to confine experience to the here and
now. I have chosen one of his earliest poems.

The Lemons

Listen to me, the poets laureate
walk only among plants

with rare names: boxwood, privet and acanthus.
But I like roads that lead to grassy
ditches where boys
scoop up a few starved
eels out of half-dry puddles:
paths that run among the banks,
come down among the tufted canes
and end in orchards, among the lemon trees.

Better if the hubbub of the birds
dies out, swallowed by the blue:
we can hear more of the whispering
of friendly branches in not-quite-quiet air,
and the sensations of this smell
that can't divorce itself from earth
and rains a restless sweetness on the heart.
Here, by some miracle, the war
of troubled passions calls a truce;
here we poor, too, receive our share of riches,
which is the fragrance of the lemons.

See, in these silences where things
give over and seem on the verge of betraying
their final secret,
sometimes we feel we're about
to uncover an error in Nature,
the still point of the world, the link that won't hold,
the thread to untangle that will finally lead
to the heart of a truth.
The eye scans its surroundings,
the mind inquires aligns divides
in the perfume that gets diffused
at the day's most languid.
It's in these silences you see
in every fleeting human
shadow some disturbed Divinity.

But the illusion fails, and time returns us
to noisy cities where the blue
is seen in patches, up between the roofs.
The rain exhausts the earth then;
winter's tedium weighs the houses down,
the light turns miserly – the soul bitter.
Till one day through a half-shut gate
in a courtyard, there among the trees,
we can see the yellow of the lemons;
And the chill in the heart
melts, and deep in us
the golden horns of sunlight
pelt their songs.

(Eugenio Montale, *Collected Poems 1920–1954*, trans. Jonathan
Galassi, New York, Farrar Strauss and Giroux, 1997, pp. 9–11)

XI

John Donne's career was nothing if not colourful. Born a
Catholic, educated by Catholic tutors, law student at Lincoln's
Inn, military service with Essex and Raleigh, he became MP for
Brackley, Northamptonshire in 1601. He was secretary to Sir
Thomas Egerton, but after secretly marrying Egerton's niece he
was passed over for a civil career, and dismissed by his patron.
There followed 14 years in the wilderness, apparently without
prospects. Donne was advised to seek ordination in the Church
of England, which he did in 1615. He had earlier abandoned
Catholicism some time in the mid 1590s. As Dean of St Paul's,
Donne was a renowned preacher and even greater poet. His
poetry is sensuous, alive, beautifully composed and particularly
given to reading aloud.

Holy Sonnet X

Death, be not proud, though some have called thee
Mighty and dreadful, for thou are not so;

For those whom thou thinkest thou dost overthrow
Die not, poor Death, nor yet canst thou kill me.
From rest and sleep, which but thy pictures be,
Much pleasure – then, from thee much more must flow;
And soonest our best men with thee do go,
Rest of their bones and soul's delivery.
Thou'rt slave to fate, chance, kings, and desperate men,
And dost with poison, war, and sickness dwell;
And poppy or charms can make us sleep as well,
And better than thy stroke. Why swellest thou then?
One short sleep past, we wake eternally,
And death shall be no more. Death, thou shalt die.

(*John Donne: Complete Poetry and Selected Prose*, edited by John
Hayward, London, The Nonesuch Press, 1929, pp. 383–4.)

XII

St John of the Cross (1542–91) was the joint founder with St
Teresa of Avila of the Discalced Carmelites. He held together
with profound resonance the precision of Thomist theology and
an imagination stirred to poetry by the wonder and excitement
of what he understood to be the threefold movement of the soul
towards God: purgation, illumination and ultimate union. His
work is not easy – how could it be since he sought to grapple
with the 'dark night of the soul'? But there is no better appre-
hension of the soul's desire for God than the aspiration of love
which St John expresses with such sensuous intelligence in his
poetry.

Upon the Gospel 'In the Beginning was the Word'
relating to the Most Holy Trinity.

In the beginning of all things
The Word lived in the Lord at rest.
And His felicity in Him
Was from infinity possessed.

That very Word was God Himself
By which all being was begun
For He lived in the beginning
And beginning had he none.

He Himself was the beginning,
So He had none, being one.
What was born of the beginning
Was the Word we call the Son.

Even so has God conceived Him
And conceived Him always so,
Ever giving Him the substance
As He gave it long ago.

And thus the glory of the Son
Is the glory of the Sire
And the Glory of the Father
From His Son He does acquire.

As the loved-one in the lover
Each in the other's heart resided:
And the love that makes them one
Into one of them divided,

Then with one and with the other
Mated in such equality,
Three Persons now and one Beloved
They numbered, though they still were three.

There is one love in all Three Persons:
One lover all the Three provides;
And the beloved is the lover
Which in each of them resides.

The Being which all three possess
Each of them does possess alone:
And each of them loves what that Being
Itself possesses of its own.

This very Being is Each One,
And it alone, in its way,
Has bound them in that wondrous knot
Whose mystery no man can say.

Thus lives undying and eternal
The love that has entwined them so,
Because one love the three united
Which as their Essence now we know,
And this one love, the more in one-ness,
The more and more in love will grow.

(St John of the Cross, *Poems*, trans. Roy Campbell,
Harmondsworth, Penguin, 1960, Romance 1, pp. 65, 67)

XIII

Neville Ward (1914–96), *Five for Sorrow, Ten for Joy*

Neville Ward was a distinguished priest and Methodist minister whose life was focused on the task of encouraging people to open their eyes to the beauty that lay about them. He was aware of all traditions of prayer, and anxious to introduce any who approached him to the whole world of spiritual aspiration. Gerard Manley Hopkins, W. B. Yeats, Marcel Proust, Beaudelaire, James Joyce and William James, together with the Bible, to name but a few, were some of the resources on which he drew for inspiration. He inhabited the whole realm of Catholic spirituality, never more so than in this book on the rosary, happily republished in 2007 by the Epworth Press.

XIV

Louis MacNiece (1907–63) was the son of an Irish priest and Bishop of Down. He met W. H. Auden and Stephen Spender when at Oxford and is frequently associated with them, though he never achieved their success. He became a BBC producer after a period when he taught the classics, and made a fine career for himself as a writer for radio. His reputation as a poet has fluctuated but *Autumn Journal* is a fine poem by any standards. These lines bear witness to the connectedness of all things and their dependence upon dynamic relationships.

In Autumn

XVII

Nothing is self-sufficient, pleasure implies hunger
    But hunger implies hope:
I cannot lie in the bath for ever, clouding
    The cooling water with rose-geranium soap.
I cannot drug my life with the present moment;
    The present moment may rape – but all in vain –
The future, for the future remains a virgin
    Who must be tried again.

XXIV

Time is a country, the present moment
    A spotlight roving round the scene;
We need not chase the spotlight,
    The future is the bride of what has been.

(Louis MacNiece, Collected Poems 1925–1948, London,
Faber and Faber, 1949, pp. 157, 173)

These are surely words to ponder over. 'The future is the bride of what has been'; I like that. Perhaps, indeed, death is the completeness which witnesses to the fact that human life is made worthwhile by love of the future that Christians believe lies in the hands of God, Father, Son and Holy Spirit.

Notes

Preface

1 Cicero, *Cicero's Letters to Atticus*, trans. with introduction by D. R. Shackleton Bailey, Harmondsworth, Penguin, 1978, p. 31.

2 Ludwig Wittgenstein, *Culture and Value*, ed. G. H. von Wright, trans. Peter Winch, Oxford, Basil Blackwell, amended second edition, 1980, p. 68e.

Chapter 1

3 See article by correspondent Tony Paterson from Berlin, *Sunday Telegraph*, London, 15 July 2007.

4 Book of Common Prayer, 1st Anthem.

5 Book of Common Prayer, 1st Anthem.

6 J-P de Caussade SJ, quoted in John McManners, *Death and the Enlightenment: Changing Attitudes to Death Among Christians and Unbelievers in Eighteenth Century France*, Oxford, Clarendon Press, 1981, p. 218.

7 From the fifteenth-century *Talbot Book of Hours*, in the Fitzwilliam Museum, Cambridge. Quoted from Eamon Duffy, *Marking the Hours*, New Haven and London, Yale University Press, 2006, p. 78

8 Dante Alighieri, *The Divine Comedy*, *Inferno*, trans. Robert Pinsky, London, J. M. Dent, 1996, Canto 1, p. 5.

9 Joseph Conrad, *Lord Jim*, Harmondsworth, Penguin Books, 1949, p. 15.

10 Ludwig Wittgenstein, *Culture and Value*, ed. G. H. von Wright, trans. Peter Winch, Oxford, Basil Blackwell, amended second edition, 1980, p. 71e.

11 Elizabeth Barrett Browning, *A Vision of Poets*, verse 100.

12 The survey was conducted by the BBC in co-operation with several other organizations and published in March 2007.

13 The dramatic reality of the situation in Zimbabwe is made plain in the following report. Someone interviewed for the press in June 2007

reported that she paid today as much for a banana as she had for her home ten years previously!

14 Isaiah 53.5. I prefer another translation 'at the cost of his wounds' which seems to me to do more justice to the feeling of the Hebrew than the rather pallid expression 'by his bruises' of the NRSV. Thus, 'Yet he was pierced for our transgressions, crushed for our iniquities; his was the chastisement that brought us weal, and at the cost of his wounds there is healing for us.' *The Second Isaiah: Introduction, Translation and Commentary to Chapters XL–LV*, Oxford, Clarendon Press, 1964, p. 64.

15 2 Corinthians 13.11. The NSRV has 'Put things in order' in place of 'Be perfect'. One cannot quibble with the translation; in a literal sense, the Greek verb means 'complete, put things together, make whole'. However, 'Be perfect', implies wholeness, completeness and is a more challenging divine perspective which is lost in the NRSV. Let's keep our nerve!

16 Wittgenstein, *Culture and Value*, p. 26e.

17 Günter Grass, *Peeling the Onion*, London, Harvill Secker, 2007, p. 153.

18 Bernard Williams, *Problems of the Self, The Makropulos Case: Reflections on the Tedium of Immortality*, Cambridge, Cambridge University Press, 1973, p. 100.

19 See below, Chapter 2.

20 Martin Heidegger, *Being and Time*, trans. John Macquarrie and Edward Robinson, Oxford, Basil Blackwell, 1973, p. 289.

21 Mary Wesley, for example, published her first novel at the pleasantly young age of 70.

22 Martin Goodman, *Rome and Jerusalem: The Clash of Ancient Civilizations*, London, Allen Lane, 2007, pp. 361–3.

23 Luke 3.23.

24 John 19.30.

25 These are the memorable words of the translation in the Authorised Version and of Evening Prayer in the Book of Common Prayer.

Chapter 2

26 The author of a most excellent book on death and dying in ancient Rome puts it like this. 'Dying is fundamentally an active rather than a passive process . . .' She goes on to say that many Latin authors '. . . share a perception of death as a privileged moment which has the capacity to reveal the true character of the dying subject'. Catherine Edwards, *Death in Ancient Rome*, New Haven and London, Yale University Press, 2007, p. 5.

27 See below, Chapter 4.

28 Ladislaus Boros, *The Moment of Truth: Mysterium Mortis*,

London, Burns and Oates, 1965, p. 165. Something of a similar point of view, though presented in a very different philosophical framework, is suggested by Lucius Annaeus Seneca, Stoic philosopher (*c.* 4 BC–65 AD) who wrote in one of his last letters, '. . . the human heart is never more divine than when it reflects on its mortality'. Seneca, *Epistulae Morales* 120.14. Quoted in Catherine Edwards, *Death in Ancient Rome*, p. 18.

29 See below, Chapter 3.

30 It is worth remarking that such grand speculation was a feature of intellectual life in the first century BC. See, for example, Lucretius, *The Nature of the Universe*, trans. R. E. Latham of *De Rerum Natura*, Harmondsworth, Penguin Books, 1951. Lucretius expressed in his fine poem an Epicurean philosophy that traced all meaning and sense to material objects: in some ways he could be said to have anticipated evolutionary theory.

31 Cf. Richard Gregory, the neuropsychologist, who replies when asked whether he believed in life after death, 'Oh, I just think one snuffs it.' Susan Blackmore, ed. *Conversations on Consciousness*, Oxford, Oxford University Press, 2005, p. 107.

32 For relevant discussion see, for example, John Bowker, *The Meanings of Death*, Cambridge, Cambridge University Press, 1991.

33 Genesis 2.15–16; 3.1–19.

34 See Chapter 6.

35 1 Corinthians 15.22.

36 Brother Lawrence, *The Practice of the Presence of God*, trans. D. Attwater, Orchard Books, Extra Series 3, 1926.

37 2 Peter 1.2–11.

38 Abbot Marmion, *Union with God*, London, Sands and Co., 1934, p. 1.

39 A most excellent book on this theme is Mark A. McIntosh, *Discernment and Truth: The Spirituality and Theology of Knowledge*, New York, Herder and Herder, 2004. It is not a 'difficult' book but, in my opinion, it is a book which merits being read slowly, and carefully digested, so that it has time to make an impact on the way one thinks and feels about Truth and the ways of apprehending it.

40 Ephesians 2.19–20.

41 For full discussion of this view see John Hick, *Evil and the God of Love*, London, 1966.

42 Charles Davis, *A Question of Conscience*, New York, Harper & Row, 1967.

43 Phillip Pullman, *His Dark Materials*, London, Scholastic Books, 1995, 1997, 2000.

44 *The Tablet*, 31 March 2007, p. 29.

45 See Chapter 5 for a discussion of human identity and the nature of that rarely discussed subject, the soul.

46 Romans 3.23.

47 Romans 6.1–4.

48 The so-called second baptism, or baptism in the Holy Spirit, is something quite different and associated primarily with churches of the Pentecostal tradition, who hold the view that the gifts of the Spirit referred to in 1 Corinthians and found in Acts are still capable of being received by true believers today. These gifts are thought to include, for example, exorcism, glossolalia and prophecy.

49 Michael Oakeshott used these terms to develop an influential approach to human experience and its interpretation over time through the means of education. Cf. Michael Oakeshott, *Experience and its Modes*, Cambridge, Cambridge University Press, 1933 (pb. 1985); *The Voice of Liberal Learning: Michael Oakeshott on Education*, ed. Timothy Fuller, New Haven and London, Yale University Press, 1989.

50 De Caussade, Pierre J-P, SJ, *Lettres Spirituelles*, ed. M. Olphe-Gaillard, SJ, 1960, p. 318.

Chapter 3

51 Hilary Putnam, *Meaning and the Moral Sciences*, London, Routledge and Kegan Paul, 1978, p. 5.

52 Plato, *Phaedo*, 118a.

53 Plato, *Apologia*, 42. trans. Hugh Tredennick.

54 Putnam, *Meaning and the Moral Sciences*, p. 85.

55 Clive Bell, *Civilisation*, first published 1928, reprinted London, Chatto and Windus, Pelham Library, 1941.

56 Heidegger was indeed a very great philosopher, perhaps with Wittgenstein one of the two greatest philosophers of the twentieth century. He was seduced by Nazism and became a supporter of Hitler, but it is as absurd to ignore the illumination provided in his philosophy for that reason as it would be to ignore Beethoven's last quartets because he was deaf when he composed them and never 'heard' them.

57 Edmund Husserl, *Ideas: General Introduction to Pure Phenomenology*, trans. W. E. R. Boyce Gibson, London, Allen and Unwin, 1931, pp. 234–7.

58 Ernst Bloch, *The Principle of Hope*, Oxford, Blackwell, 3 vols, 1954–9.

59 Jürgen Moltmann, *The Theology of Hope*, London, SCM Press, 1967.

60 Thomas Torrance, *Theological Science*, London, Oxford University Press, 1969.

61 *The Hope of Salvation for Infants Who Die Without Being Baptised*, Report of the Vatican Theological Commission accepted by

Pope Benedict in January 2007. Fr Paul McPartlan said, 'We cannot say we know with certainty what will happen to unbaptised children but we have good grounds to hope that God in his mercy and love looks after these children and brings them to salvation.'

62 For an elegant discussion of this point, see Keith Ward, *Religion and Revelation*, Oxford, Clarendon Press, 1994, pp. 3–36.

63 Paul Rorem, *Pseudo-Dionysius: A Commentary on the Texts and an Introduction to their Influence*, New York, Oxford University Press, 1993.

64 Abbot Marmion, *Union with God*, Sands & Co., 2nd impression, 1949, p. 1.

65 Bede, *Homilies on the Gospels*, Corpus Christianorum, p. 122. ET by L. T. Martin and D. Hurst, 2 vols, Cistercian Studies 110–11, Kalamazoo, 1991, quoted in Gordon Mursell, *English Spirituality*, Vol. 1, *From Earliest Times to 1700*, London, SPCK, 2001, p. 56.

Chapter 4

66 E. L. Mascall, *The Christian Universe*, London, Darton, Longman and Todd, 1968. As to the vastness of the dimensions of Mascall's Christian universe, I've not yet worked out to my own satisfaction what exactly he's getting at when he talks of angels!

67 J. B. Phillips, *Your God is Too Small*, London, Epworth Press, 1962.

68 Ludwig Wittgenstein, *Tractatus Logico–Philosophicus*, London, Routledge and Kegan Paul, 1961, 6.4311.

69 Matthew 26.39.

70 Ladislaus Boros, *The Moment of Truth*, London, Burns & Oates, 1962, p. 2.

71 Martin Heidegger, *Being and Time*, Oxford, Basil Blackwell, 1962, p. 286.

72 Dylan Thomas, *Collected Poems 1934–1952*, 'Do not go gentle into that good night', London, J. M. Dent, 1952, p. 116.

73 Nicholas Humphrey, *Seeing Red: A Study in Consciousness*, Cambridge, Mass., and London, The Belknap Press of Harvard University, 2006, p. 113.

74 Pope John XXIII, *Journal of a Soul*, London, Geoffrey Chapman, 1964, Appendix 6, p. 448.

75 *The Book of the Craft of Dying* (fifteenth century, from either Latin or possibly French sources), quoted by Gordon Mursell, *English Spirituality*, Vol. 1, *From Earliest Times to 1700*, London, SPCK, 1981, p. 199.

Chapter 5

76 *Hymns Ancient and Modern New Standard*, London, Hymns Ancient and Modern Limited, 15th impression, 2000, No. 192. *Hymns and Psalms*, Peterborough, Methodist Publishing House, 1983, No. 13.

77 *Hymns and Psalms*, No. 180. *Hymns Ancient and Modern New Standard*, No. 67 (verse 4 is omitted in *Hymns Ancient and Modern*, and verse 5, line 2 has the original 'offering' replaced by 'present' in *Hymns and Psalms*).

78 Daniel Dennett in Susan Blackmore, ed. *Conversations on Consciousness*, Oxford, Oxford University Press, 2005, p. 82.

79 Richard Dawkins, *The God Delusion*, London, Bantam Press, 2006, p. 359.

80 Rene Descartes, *The Passions of the Soul*, in *The Philosophical Writings of Descartes*, Vol. 1, trans. John Cottingham, Robert Stoothoff and Dugald Murdoch, Cambridge, Cambridge University Press, 1985, pp. 339–40.

81 The association of Christianity with apocalyptic certainties, which has occurred from time to time, is political reductionism of a most disturbing kind. It is most unfortunately all too current in the visions of President Bush and Tony Blair, not to mention the horrors of Nazism, fundamentalist Islam and communism. For a clear discussion of this theme, see John Gray, *Black Mass*, Allen Lane, 2007.

82 For a most stimulating discussion of the issues involved in this question, see Richard E. Creel, *Divine Impassibility: An Essay in Philosophical Theology*, Cambridge, Cambridge University Press, 1986.

83 The weed can destroy concrete, undermine buildings and unmake roads, quite apart from what it does to your garden if you are unfortunate enough to be invaded by it. The rhizomes of the Japanese knotweed can penetrate for several metres and also reproduce vegetatively from any fragment of the plant. Removing all traces of it can take several years.

84 John A. T. Robinson, *Honest to God*, London, SCM Press, 1963.

85 John 19.30.

86 Genesis 1.31.

87 Walter Brueggemann, *Theology of the Old Testament: Testimony, Dispute, Advocacy*, Minneapolis, Fortress Press, 1997, *passim* but especially Part III, pp. 407–564.

88 Blackmore, *Conversations on Consciousness*.

89 Sebastian Moore, *God is a New Language*, London, Longman and Todd, 1967.

90 For a full discussion see Nicholas Humphrey, *Seeing Red: A Study in Consciousness*, Cambridge, Mass., and London, The Belknap Press of Harvard University, 2006.

91 Humphrey, *Seeing Red*, p. 70. The italics in the quotation are in the original.

92 Humphrey, *Seeing Red*, p. 128.

Chapter 6

93 I have in mind here such terms as 'force', 'number', 'conscious-ness'; they are products of the ways in which the human mind organizes experience so as to be able to make sense of it and discuss it with others. One may argue, and I probably would, that the term 'God' functions in much the same way; it is a term which most human societies have employed in order to embody their interpretative response to their experience in a story which holds together all their experience in whatever form it arises, so as to explore it by sharing it and conversing about it with others.

94 John R. Searle, *Freedom and Neurobiology*, New York, Columbia University Press, 2007, chapter 2, 'Social Ontology and Political Power', pp. 79–109. John R. Searle, *The Construction of Social Reality*, London, Allen Lane, 1995.

95 Samuel Taylor Coleridge, *Biographia Literaria* (1817), London, J. M. Dent and Sons Ltd (Everyman's Library Edition), 1956, ch. xiv, pp. 173.4.

96 Herman Melville, *Moby Dick*, Oxford, Oxford University Press, 1998.

97 Sebastian Faulks, *Birdsong*, London, Hutchinson, 1993.

98 Barbara Kingsolver, *The Poisonwood Bible*, London, Faber and Faber, 1998.

99 Wayne Booth, *The Rhetoric of Fiction*, Chicago, The University of Chicago Press, 2nd edition, 1983.

100 Kenneth Wilson, *Learning to Hope*, Peterborough, Epworth, 2005, p. vii.

101 Pope John XXIII, *Journey of a Soul*, London, Geoffrey Chapman, 1965, p. 342.

102 Charles Wesley, *Hymns and Psalms*, London, Methodist Publishing House, 1983, No. 528.

Chapter 7

103 Quoted in the anonymous obituary of Richard Rorty in the *Daily Telegraph*, Monday 11 June 2007.

104 Emmanuel Kant, *Critique of Pure Reason*, 1781, Cambridge, Cambridge University Press, 1998, Preface to the first edition, pp. 100–1.

105 Tim Blanning, *The Pursuit of Glory: Europe 1648–1815*, London, Allen Lane, 2007, p. 520. It is worth noting that when reading much of contemporary sociology of religion one is aware of a subtle ability to *describe* with illuminating accuracy the outward forms of religious life and the personal behaviour of religious believers, but its failure to get at the heart of religion. It frequently lacks sensitivity to the inner reality of the holy mystery that enchants believers and gives them life. It is as if the sociologist is unable, and perhaps unwilling, to grasp the reality of the liturgy that is performed in the sanctuary. See Kieran Flanagan, *Sociology and Liturgy: Re-presentations of the Holy*, London, Macmillan, 1991; Kieran Flanagan, *The Enchantment of Sociology, A Study of Sociology and Culture*, London, Macmillan, 1996.

106 Psalm 34.8.

107 John 11.25–6.

108 John 11.1–57, esp. 1–44.

109 For the evidence regarding Shakespeare's provenance see A. D. Nuttall, *Shakespeare The Thinker*, New Haven and London, Yale University Press, 2007, pp. 12–22.

110 I was living in North Wales at the time: my comment is based upon personal conversation.

111 Orthodoxy does not lay the same emphasis on the definition of the Seven Sacraments as does Roman Catholicism; interestingly, for example, it is inclined to regard the funeral service as a sacrament.

112 As every Sunday School teacher knows, in contrast to our tradition where the shepherd follows the flock, the shepherd leads his flock in the Near East, to search out danger and protect the flock.

113 Psalm 23.4.

114 John 6.35–40.

115 John 14.27.

116 A funeral may, however, be a sacramental. A sacramental disposes the faithful to receive the benefits of the faith celebrated in the sacramental life; it may take the form of blessings of meals, objects, persons, or places and is a reminder of God's holy presence in the Creation suffused by God's Spirit.

117 For illuminating discussion of the text and its history, see John S. Lampard, *Go Forth, Christian Soul: The Biography of a Prayer*, Peterborough, Epworth, 2005. Lampard offers a translation of the whole of the *Nursia* text on pp. 2–4. The words are those of John Henry Newman as used by Elgar in *The Dream of Gerontius*.

Epilogue

118 *The Oxford Companion to English Literature* (new edition), Margaret Drabble, ed., Oxford, 1985, s.v. *In memoriam A.H.H.*

119 Sword-rune, 'If thy heart fail thee trust not in me'.

Acknowledgements

The author and publisher acknowledge the following sources for extract material under copyright. Permission has been applied for.

Thomas Blackburn, *Post Mortem*, Rondo Publications Ltd, 1977.

Eugenio Montale, *Collected Poems 1920–1954*, Farrar, Strauss and Giroux, 1998.

Pablo Neruda, *100 Love Sonnets*, University of Texas Press, 1996.

Ezra Pound, *Selected Poems*, David Higham Associates for Faber and Faber, (1928), reprint of 1964.